THROUGH THE EYES OF SPIRIT

To Elaine,

May you be blessed

with goodhealth, love

and laughter always.
You are an earth angel!

Much love & Many Blessings

Jenny Crawford

x⁺ᵗᛘₓˣ

Through the Eyes
of Spirit

Jennifer Christine Crawford

Blue Dolphin Publishing
1996

Published by Blue Dolphin Publishing, Inc.
P.O. Box 8, Nevada City, CA 95959
Orders: 1-800-643-0765

ISBN: 0-931892-32-5

Library of Congress Cataloging-in-Publication Data

Crawford, Jennifer Christine, 1955–
    Through the eyes of spirit / Jennifer Christine Crawford.
        p.   cm.
    ISBN 0-931892-32-5 (pbk.)
    1. Spiritualism.   2. Crawford, Jennifer Christine, 1955–
3. Mediums—Biographhjy.   I. Title.
    BF1261.2.C73 1996
    133.9—dc20   96-30461
                                                                         CIP

Cover art: John Krajewski

Printed in the United States of America by
Blue Dolphin Press, Inc., Grass Valley, California.

5   4   3   2   1

Dedication

THIS BOOK is dedicated to God and those in the spirit world, for blessing me with a special gift and for giving me the strength to share this gift with humanity, helping to share and extend spiritual love, healing, understanding, and light.

To my loving husband, Robert: without your editing skills, love, wisdom, strength, and patience, this book would not have been possible. Thank you for all your support. I love you, darling, with all my heart.

To both our families, especially my Mum, Anneliese, and to our close links in the spirit world: Ken, Jacquie, Ian, Jack, and others. We love you all.

To all our friends in New Zealand, Kauai, Oahu, Hawaii, Laguna Beach, and other parts of the United States, Canada, Australia, and England, who have shown us so much love and kindness.

To those in the spirit world, for watching over us: thank you for giving me the inspiration and guidance to write this book, and thank you for making the stars shine brightly when the sky seemed grey.

Love and blessings to you all—the lights of my life.

Table of Contents

Acknowledgments

M<small>Y ETERNAL THANKS</small> to Rob for cooking me all those lovely meals. Thank you for the countless hours you spent working on this book—my eternal soulmate.

My love and thanks to two beautiful people: Sue Phillipson, friend and artist, and Jill Marie Landis, friend and national bestselling author. You both walk with such a bright light around you. Thank you both for the countless hours we spent in discussion and for your encouragement and help. But most of all, thanks for your love and belief in me; without your faith we might not have completed this project.

To Joan Conrow, journalist and writer: thank you for your friendship and unconditional love on the island of Kauai.

To Anne: without your love and support, our message may have taken much more time to spread; thank you for believing in us.

To the mediums who helped so much in setting and guiding me on my spiritual pathway: Elma Farmer, Maureen Chapman, and Phyllis Tantrum—all great mediums.

My love and eternal thanks to you all.

Introduction

So many people ask me *how* I got started as a medium, and *when* I recognized that I had spiritual and psychic gifts. The gifts were already in me, but undeveloped.

At an early age I sensed that I was in some way different than the other children around me. I always felt a strong presence with me. I could not explain why I felt different from the other children, but as my early years flew by, my differences became much clearer to me. As a young child I often remember looking over my shoulder to see who was standing behind me. The "presence" with me always felt very strong and very comfortable.

I was to learn later in life that this presence was my very own spirit guide, who would talk to me and give me the vital guidance and direction required to communicate with the spirit world.

A spirit guide is a person assigned to us from the spirit world to teach and guide us through life. Our spirit guides are evolved souls who have a high level of conscious awareness. They operate within a higher vibration. Some mediums may also refer to a person's spirit guide as their spiritual Angel.

Despite being a medium, I consider myself a very ordinary person. The gift that I have been given is sometimes very hard to talk about, as linking with the spirit world comes so naturally to me. I feel that having an expansive and alert mind is one of the qualities that helps me to make strong communications with the spirit world.

The best way to describe or explain how a person becomes a medium is to say that one is born this way. A medium communicates with and talks to persons or souls, whom we refer to collectively as "Spirit," who are very much alive in the spiritual realms or spirit world. We do not bother spirit. Rather, they approach us to link with their loved ones who are on the earth plane. Mediumship is a gift given by God. We are selected by the highest power to become a medium, and the work of mediumship requires a commitment to God, a lifetime commitment of serving humanity. It is doubly important for mediums to balance their psychic and spiritual gifts and develop them together; this enables them to work with people in a loving and caring manner.

This job entails the utmost responsibility and integrity. Our commitment must be one of helping to heal people on this planet, of making our world and environment a much better place for all. We must spread the light, always sharing the light and linking hearts together in love.

I serve as a middleman or interpreter between the spirit world and those living on the earth plane. I am often called upon by people on the earth plane to make a link with their loved ones in the spirit world. Making such connections enables me to bring forward proof of life beyond death. The communication I make with the spirit world is like having a friendly chat with a person, except for the fact that the person I am chatting with is "visible" and "audible" in a spiritual sense rather than physically. The chatting carries on silently in my head while I am talking to those in the spirit world, and then, once I have received a message, I pass it on to the person sitting with me.

I work clairvoyantly and clairaudiently. Clairvoyance is being able to see in my mind a vision of the person in the spirit world and how they looked when they were alive on the earth plane. Clairaudience is being able to hear a person's voice talking to me from the spirit world; I will also hear whether that person has an accent or not.

To link with the spirit world, I have to raise my vibration to a higher level, which is like turning on a switch within my energy field. I sit quietly and still my mind. I feel as though the top of my head opens up like a flower, and when I have finished communicating with the spirit world, I visualize the flower above my head closing up again. This enables a clear connection of communication between the spirit world, myself, and the loved one sitting in front of me. My spiritual guides help to raise my level of consciousness to enable each connection to take place.

As one might expect, many people approach me for advice, reassurance, and guidance. Many people come to see me in order to make a special link with a loved one who has passed over to the spirit world. I call this a reading. Also, as an extension of my work as a medium, I have a dream of sharing my spiritual pathway with those already enlightened and with those seeking to develop their awareness.

No one told me in the beginning that I had the gift to be called a medium. As it turned out, I had to be prompted by spirit to begin calling myself a medium. It happened like this: I was invited to attend a spiritual meeting when I was in my late twenties, and some of us at the meeting were asked to stand up and give spiritual messages to others. This came very naturally to me. The speaker also asked that after we each gave our messages, we let the audience know what we called ourselves: healers, psychics, or mediums. A lady sitting beside me stood up and announced very confidently to the audience that she was a medium. The messages she had just completed giving to the audience were terrible—full of doom and gloom. It seemed to me as though she was not connecting to the higher spiritual realms, from where clear and loving messages are constantly relayed. In fact, no one could understand the information she was passing on. It was as though she was making it all up. I could not believe that she had introduced herself as a medium. This really made me stand up. If she is a medium, I thought, I'll eat my hat. When it came to my turn to introduce myself, I still was not quite sure what to say, but my spirit guide knew better, and before I could think about what to say, the words came out of my mouth in a loud and clear voice. I announced I was a medium. The lady beside me glared at me in disbelief at hearing my introduction. I felt filled with joy as I made this announcement, and a deep smile emerged from within. The lady came up to me after the meeting had finished and asked me how I thought I was qualified to call myself a medium. Without hesitation I said to her, "I am a medium, my dear, because I link with the spirit world and pass messages on with love in my heart." I told her that I truly believed in the work I was doing, and that I found such wonderful solace and light associated with my work. Since then I have never doubted this title.

Over the years I have had many visions from the spirit world, which have given me confidence, strength, and a sense of direction with my work. One vision I received in my sleep state was particularly powerful, and I would like to share this vision with you. I had been asking for strong guidance from the spirit world as to the direction my spiritual work would take me.

As I lay sleeping, I was shown a vision of the three wise men from Bethlehem. They seemed as though their whole beings were filled with pure love. As I looked at them, they spoke to me and told me not to worry, that all would be well, and then they pointed to a bright star in the sky. "This is the star of Bethlehem," they told me, "the star that will always shine brightly for you." They went on to tell me that they had shown me this star so that I would share this bright light and help to guide and give others direction throughout their lives, via spiritual teachings. When I awoke the next morning, I felt filled with a glorious light, and this vision gave me a sense of peace and contentment. I knew then that I should never doubt the power and wisdom given to me from the spirit world to continue my work as a medium. I realized then without a doubt that I had been given this gift to share and to serve. I literally become the medium or communication channel used by the spirit world to pass on relevant information from spirit to those on the earth plane.

It is a medium's job to give as much proof of survival in the life hereafter as possible. A medium works with people, giving them messages from the spirit world and information that only they understand and no one else could possibly know about. This has been proven to me many times over, and this will be covered more extensively later in the book.

Throughout this book I would like to talk to you about life as a medium and share many warm, loving, and personal experiences with you. Death is not the end of our existence, and I would like to share many experiences that prove this fact. I pray that this book will touch many hearts with messages of love, healing, and blessings from the spirit world.

CHAPTER ONE

Walking in the Light

IT WAS IN 1990, during a quiet moment of personal meditation, that I had a wonderful, light experience. This meditation was one of the most powerful and loving experiences I have ever had from spirit. As I lay still in meditation, I saw the most beautiful, angelic face looking at me, a face that had tremendous warmth and love to it. It was a man's face, a face that had the most beautiful, crystal-clear, blue eyes, like none I had ever seen before, and which shone like glistening diamonds. These were healing eyes. I felt a strong recognition within myself that this person was truly from a higher dimension and that my life had been touched in an extraordinary way. My whole being became filled with the most glorious light, a light that engulfed me with healing, joy, and upliftment. Ever since then, whenever I think of this being's face, especially those beautiful eyes, I am filled again with feelings of overpowering warmth and love.

I came to realize that I was receiving many visions of light, and that this light was given to me to draw upon and pass on to others. This was a spiritual light that would give me energy and strength and be with me throughout my time here on the earth plane.

These continuing light experiences changed my life and put me on the true pathway of my spiritual work. These experiences, I now realize, were given to me as a blessing "through the eyes of spirit." The bright light given to me has seemed to serve as a beacon to draw in those people to see me who need some light to brighten their pathways.

I believe there are many light workers throughout the world who have been sent to counteract the negativity and darkness that often manifests itself around us here on the earth plane. The light workers are those people who really care about humanity and Mother Earth. As we walk a good strong spiritual pathway, we learn to link with spiritual light and share it with others. We all desire a much improved world to live in, and to live our lives in peace, safety, and harmony. As light-workers, we all strive for a better world for our children. It is up to us to instigate change by constantly thinking positive thoughts and sending out positive energy. By practicing this in our day-to-day lives, our thoughts become strong projections, sending out this light to others. By linking with and having the courage to follow our spiritual pathways, we allow ourselves to become beacons that travel throughout the world, sharing love, light, and a new awareness.

Many of us have light workers in our families, and I am no exception, since I inherited some of my spiritual gifts from my Jewish grandfather.

CHAPTER TWO

The Journey Begins

MY GRANDFATHER WAS BORN in Germany. He was very psychic, and I inherited some of his gifts. I believe that in most generations there will be at least one family member who has a strong psychic ability; that person will often be remembered by other members of the family for some of the predictions they had made.

My Jewish grandfather could see the future for Germany, prior to the outbreak of World War II. He knew he had to leave Berlin before the Nazis came to his door. He tried, with little success, to convince many family members that he could see into the future. He told his relatives, "You must get out of Germany now, or it will cost you your lives."

"How do you know this?" they asked.

The simple answer to this question was, of course, that my grandfather was extremely psychic. He was a gentleman of average height, slim build, well-dressed, and he always wore a well-cut suit. He had strong, striking features. His psychic gifts were perhaps difficult for others to understand.

He managed to escape the Nazis, taking my mother with him, along with a few other family members. After going into hiding for several months after their escape, my grandfather and my mother eventually ended up in New Zealand.

On one occasion, returning home from the theatre not long before they fled, they sighted a Gestapo car parked outside their home. They drove straight past and spent the night with friends. My grandfather knew it was time to leave.

They managed to leave Berlin, taking only a few personal possessions with them and leaving the house intact, as if they had been going for a family outing and planning to return the same day.

My mother also inherited her father's psychic gifts, although she never spoke very much about the subject until I was much older. Eventually, I brought up the subject and began to share many experiences with my mother in my adult years.

My father was of Scottish/Irish heritage, and he was raised as an orphan. I believe I inherited psychic gifts from both sides of my family. My father always called me his "golden girl" throughout his life; perhaps it was a name given to him by spirit; I'm not sure. It always made me feel good when he called me by that name. I also have a brother-in-law, Doug, who always calls me "sunshine." Such nicknames can be so meaningful and encouraging, perhaps because they reflect a spiritual essence.

At times I found it hard during my school years to link with teachers who had different vibrations than myself. Being a sensitive, I used to drift away in a meditative state of mind during a class that had subjects I found hard to relate to, or more to the point, that I wasn't interested in.

I would just sit quietly in class, stilling my mind, and feel myself drifting out of my body. Reflecting back on that time now, I wonder what my teachers thought, looking at me and the hazy look in my eyes. So many children drift off like this, just going into that dreamy state, a half-meditative state, where we are not completely grounded. I always tell young people to imagine that their feet have the roots of a tree attached to them, or that they have spikes coming from their feet, to keep them grounded. It was very easy, I found, to come back into my body when the lesson was over, but needless to say, it didn't help my school work. How I managed to get average marks I'll never know.

People who call themselves sensitives are born this way. Some sensitives may feel as though they have a soft, absorbent shell of emotions, and they may feel a strong need for protection from others' emotions. In other words, they pick up other people's feelings very quickly. Sensitive people often find themselves working in jobs where they give great service to humanity. They also tend to absorb all information given to them, whether good or bad, and therefore need to develop discrimination along with protection. Sensitives are very spiritual people. Many sensitives develop into wonderful healers.

When you have a sensitive child, you may become aware of this fact very quickly, just by their reaction to other children around them and how they adjust to their schooling. Sensitives tend to need more loving and nurturing; they need to be taken by the hand and given strong reassurances, especially in their early years.

It seemed that even in my earlier years I was searching for something beyond the ordinary, in notions connected with the paranormal. Obviously, timing works very strongly in our spiritual development, and as a young child, I lacked the maturity needed to understand my inner emotions or feelings.

When I was about eight, my older sister Marg and I decided to hold a seance in our bedroom using a Ouija board. Innocently, we wanted to dabble but did not understand anything about the subject. We procured a glass jar to use as a pointer, pulled the curtains shut, lit a candle, and started our spooky game. It was airy and exciting. Years later I would understand the dangers involved in dabbling with Ouija boards without any prayer of protection. As people start to work with Ouija boards, they are trying to call in the spirits. This is all fine, except that they do not know whether they are calling in the good spirits or the bad spirits. Spirits reside on different levels, and this we call the higher spiritual planes or the lower level planes. The spirits who reside on the lower planes are not evolved souls. In other words, they may have been criminals or, in a word, bad people. The spirits who reside on the higher planes have conducted their lives in an honest way and have earned a place in the higher realms. With Ouija boards, it takes a good strong medium to control this sort of thing. The medium will make sure that only the spirits from the higher realms are invited to make contact through the Ouija board. I personally find it much easier just to talk with the spirits and as an adult have never been inclined to dabble in such methods.

However, we girls continued our little seance, the room seemed to fill with an air of heaviness and the candle started to flicker madly. As we were only young children, we felt frightened by this sudden change of atmosphere. I said to Marg, "Shall we stop," and she agreed that this would be a good idea. As we were about to stop, the glass jar we were using flew off the Ouija board as though someone had picked it up and dropped it. It smashed into small pieces, sending shattered glass everywhere. We never dabbled after that.

Years later, my sister Marg became more convinced of the life hereafter. She was staying with us at our home in Tauranga and got up to go to the bathroom in the wee hours of the morning. As she walked into the hallway, she saw a lady standing in an old-fashioned dress with her hair pinned up in a bun. As she was a little sleepy, she thought it may have been me, but when she spoke to the lady standing in the hallway, there was no reply. The lady just looked at her and kept smiling. Marg froze as she realized that this was, as she called it, a ghost. She let out a scream and the apparition disappeared. She has never doubted the life hereafter since. But I must admit, she slept the next night at our mum's house.

When I was thirteen years of age and in my first year of high school, I felt very lonely, as there did not seem to be any one particular girl I could connect with at an all-girls' school. I remember just sending out a thought one day about meeting a new friend. That is when a new girl came to school. Her name was Andi, and we were to become the best of friends, both sharing the pleasure of being bridesmaid and matron of honor at one another's wedding. I was to learn later on that we have no need to feel lonely or alone, as our spiritual guides walk with us throughout life always.

Always I felt as though someone was looking over my shoulder. I realized later that this was my guardian angel. Our guardian angels are our spiritual guides, assigned to us from the spirit world. They inspire us; they try to protect us, give us encouragement and upliftment in times of need, but most of all they generate love toward us, filling our whole being. I like to encourage people to remember to keep themselves open and receptive to being filled with this radiant love that spirit showers on us, even before we ask—and especially during times of need.

I left school at the age of fifteen to begin a career that would lead me to meet people who would be instrumental in guiding me on my spiritual pathway.

CHAPTER THREE

My Spiritual Pathway Is Found

AT THE AGE OF EIGHTEEN I was invited to my first spiritualist meeting by a friend called Norma, a lady I had only just met. She was going to a spiritualist meeting to hear a medium called Elma Farmer give an address and also give a clairvoyant demonstration.

"I've heard she's wonderful," she told me. "She talks to the spirits. Everyone is talking about her and her husband Ken; they work together and are a very powerful couple."

Something came over me when she mentioned this meeting. I had never heard of such meetings, and I certainly did not know what a medium was, let alone a clairvoyant demonstration. I felt filled with excitement and joy, and it made me feel all tingly inside. I felt strongly that I must attend this meeting. I wondered what was going to happen at the meeting and was filled with apprehension and excitement as we entered the hall.

I saw a lady standing at the front of the hall; she had shiny, silver hair, not a hair out of place, and was wearing a smart blue dress. She looked so serene and yet had a strong sense of power around her.

As I looked at her, she smiled at me, and her smile filled me with love and healing. I saw a bright, golden light around her head and her shoulders. I wondered if she was the medium.

Sure enough, as the meeting began, I discovered she was Elma Farmer, the medium. She opened the meeting with a short address, of which I don't remember a word, as I was so caught up by all the light that was being radiated from her. I couldn't take my eyes off her, she was so beautiful.

As she turned her attention toward the side of the hall where my friend and I were sitting, she said, "I want to come to the young lady sitting at the back of the hall," and she pointed to me. "Yes, you dear," she said.

I felt my face flush up, but at the same time I couldn't wait to hear what she had to say. I sat there spellbound, my mouth wide open, as I received my very first spiritual message from a medium. She brought my Jewish grandfather through, describing him beautifully and giving me his name. I just couldn't believe it. Even though I had only met my grandfather a few times as a young girl, I remembered him in my mind so clearly. The message I received from my grandfather was clear and very brief. He told Elma to tell me that I was a very psychic young lady and that he wanted me to pursue my spiritual pathway. I found his message to be one of encouragement, warmth, and love. Also it was a message that opened the door to my spiritual pathway.

From then on, I couldn't get to the meetings quickly enough. I hounded Elma for private readings. She would often say, "Leave it for two or three months, dear; you don't need another reading yet." But I felt so strongly that I needed the spiritual connection. She was such a positive lady, and so dynamic. If she had something to say, she would say it, but in such a spiritual way. Her messages to me from the spirit world were always so profound and encouraging, and I wanted to spend as much time with her as she would allow. I was searching for soul food, and through Elma I was being fed.

Eventually, she became my spiritual mother and teacher.

I remember on one occasion visiting Elma for a reading, and she gave me messages that were completely channelled to her from the spirit world. The messages were once again about my spiritual development and the work ahead.

Elma is a trance medium. And being a trance medium allows her spirit guides to speak directly through her to the other person. I had never experienced this before and was completely overwhelmed by the feeling of love that filled the room. Elma took only a few moments to raise her level of consciousness to allow the channelling to take place. She sat quietly in a comfortable arm chair, closed her eyes, concentrated, and all of a sudden a different voice was speaking to me. It is such a wonderful privilege to see a medium go into a state of trance; their spirit guides will allow this channeling to take place only if the person receiving the messages is worthy of seeing this gift. Elma was later to teach me how to develop my own gifts as a medium who channels. When a trance medium channels, the spirit who chooses them usually does so because the medium's voice box physically holds the correct vibration for them to speak through.

For those who have learned to see with their third eye, or psychic eye, which is in the middle of their forehead, they will often see the trance medium's face change shape as they leave their bodies and allow the spirit connection to enter. Also, a subtle change of personality will be noticed. This work is safely practiced only by mediums who are very experienced in this field. It is very dangerous for mediums to leave their bodies completely. If they do not have the correct control, then the silver cord can be severed while they are having an out-of-body experience, and they will not be able to come back. In other words, they could die.

When I am channelling, I do not leave my body completely and do not know whether I would ever be able to or want to completely let go. This takes years of practice, and only a few mediums are fully qualified as trance mediums.

I have been asked on many occasions how I discovered my psychic gifts. The discovery of my gifts was made from long periods of learning, gained from sitting with a development group. A spiritual development group is often called a circle. In such a circle, a group of people meet under the guidance of a medium to sit together and develop their psychic and spiritual gifts. Often the chairs are set in a circle.

Elma was our group leader, and if any of us had any questions concerning spiritual matters, she would readily answer them for us. Her answers were always very positive and direct. She had been a medium for a number of years and knew her subject well. This gave the group members a lot of guidance and confidence to develop their individual awarenesses.

Elma asked me if I would like to join her spiritualist group, or development circle, as she called it, which met every Monday evening. I attended those meetings for over five years, learning and gaining a great deal of knowledge every time I went.

Her development circle was just that, a group of people who could learn from one another and teach one another. But the most fascinating aspect of the group was that it was being run by Elma, a very disciplined leader, who would never allow the group to dissipate into idle chit chat. She constantly reminded us that our time linking with spirit is very precious and should never be frittered away.

We all met for a reason; it was a spiritual purpose, for healing and for developing our spiritual and psychic awareness. We always started the evening with an opening prayer, a prayer of protection. Elma would ask for God's golden band of light to be placed around all those in the group and that they be protected.

"We encourage only positive energy into our group," Elma would say. Then we would begin by placing some chairs in the middle of the circle and giving spiritual healing to one another. We simply placed our hands on a person's shoulders, or perhaps around their head area (and then be guided by spirit as to where else to place our hands); we would also say a little prayer and ask to be used as healing channels so that we could pass on upliftment to those receiving the healing.

It was not always necessary to place our hands physically on a person, as they could receive healing by our hands being held just above their heads.

In a development group I was to run several years later, one young man in this group had suffered serious injuries and was confined to a wheelchair. I asked him to give a pregnant lady some healing as he sat behind her chair in his wheelchair. He had never done this before.

He said to me, "I can't lift my hands to give her healing."

"Never mind," I said. "Just close your eyes and concentrate on giving this lady healing." As I watched and he closed his eyes and concentrated, she sat in her chair and went off into a gentle sleep.

When she drifted back, she said she felt that a pair of warm hands had been placed on her back, and she felt she had received wonderful healing. The young man said he visualized his hands being placed on her back and asked spirit to give her healing where it was required.

At the conclusion of these spiritual healing sessions in Elma's group, we would offer a prayer of absent healing for all loved ones whom we felt needed to receive the overflow of energy.

We always engaged in the healing session at the commencement of the evening, as this would lift the energy and vibration of the group.

Then we would go into a meditation, sometimes a guided meditation, or we would be given a subject to meditate upon. Sometimes we were given the subject of walking in a garden of tranquillity together or walking along the beach, perhaps following a mountain pathway or going into the redwood forest, sitting under a shady tree, or visiting a large waterfall. For example, if we meditated on visiting a large waterfall, we would have the opportunity to swim safely in this waterfall during our meditation, and some of the group members may have gained needed cleansing from this experience. Each subject could be expanded by the individual person meditating. This meditation period would sometimes last twenty minutes. Elma would never meditate with us, as she would keep an eye on the group, and bring us back after our meditation time was over, so we could share our experiences briefly together. The sharing was always very interesting.

I remember meditating in the group one Monday night when Elma played some Strauss waltz music. I found the music uplifting and invigorating and could visualize myself dancing to the music, dressed in the appropriate costume for that era!

One meditation I regularly had was visiting a native American village. I was often asked to sit with the elders and smoke the medicine pipe. The village always felt so familiar to me, as though I had been there before in another lifetime. The people, the costumes they wore, the animals, the river surrounding the village, and the trees always appeared to me with such clarity. I always returned from this meditation feeling as though I had received a great boost of healing, and this healing seemed to fill me for days afterwards.

We would next proceed to develop our psychic awareness through psychometry. At the beginning of the evening, as we entered the meeting, we all would have placed a piece of jewelry on a covered tray, not knowing each other's piece. As we came to the psychometry part of the evening, Elma would pass the tray around, and each member would select a piece of jewelry from the tray, and "tuning in," we would link with the vibrations of that particular article. We were asked to focus on a past scene, a health condition, two female names, two male names, two months of the year, and something for the future.

Then we would be given a pen and paper, write our name and the date at the top of the paper, and tune into the relevant information, writing down all our impressions to give to the person to whom the jewelry belonged. Elma always asked that we each bring an article that we knew the history of; otherwise, when giving feedback to one another, we would not know how accurate the information was. Elma has since written a book called *Psychometry: A New Way to Tune In.*

As our circle neared the end of the meeting, we would be given the opportunity of tuning into spirit, to give one another a spiritual message. It was on one such occasion that I received a message I could not readily understand. The message was, "One of them is leaving you soon," and I remember thinking, "Oh, dear God, please don't let anything happen to Elma or Ken, our teachers." But alas, within the following six weeks, Ken was to discover he had cancer, and despite all efforts and natural health remedies (Ken was an iridologist and naturopath), the body would not cure. Previous years of using sprays as a nurseryman had poisoned his system. Sadly for Elma and so many of their friends, it was Ken's time. Six weeks later, Ken was called over to the spirit world, where he continues, I am sure, to teach his strong beliefs of introducing alternative medicines.

During the night of his passing, he came to me in my sleep state, to say good-bye. I saw him, well again; in fact, he was going outside to take their dog Suzie for a walk.

He just smiled at me, as I saw him walk out of their home. "See you later, dear," he said to me.

I phoned Elma the next morning, and, sure enough, Ken had passed during the night.

The group often got messages of great upliftment for its members, and in so doing, we all felt as though we were receiving a whole week's supply of soul food. We would close the group with a prayer asking God to break our golden band of protection and send a piece home with each member of the group for the coming week to share with their families.

The five years spent with Elma Farmer and her development circle gave me a great understanding of this type of work. It has enabled me later to commence several development groups of my own, which in turn have provided many with an introduction to their own spiritual pathway.

I felt that my spiritual pathway had commenced and now look back on the experiences in Elma's circle as being my first classroom.

CHAPTER FOUR

The Work of the Channel

I SEE PEOPLE FROM ALL WALKS OF LIFE, but it is people who have had tragic loss around them that brings home the real message of my work. To me, the true work of a medium is to link these people with their loved ones in the spirit world, to provide them with peace of mind, hope, and encouragement to continue with their lives on the earth plane, knowing that their loved ones in the spirit world have gone on and are safe, well, and happy

I call myself a medium, the person who is the channel allowing spiritual messages to flow from loved ones in the spirit world to their loved ones here on the earth plane.

When I refer to "doing a reading for someone," this does not mean I am reading tarot cards or reading a person's mind. A reading means that a person or a couple have come to me and have given myself and the spirit world permission to "tune in" for them. As a channel, we sit together quietly, facing one another, and allow the energy to flow. I recommend that people record their readings, so that they can always look back and check on what has been said, whether it is in two months time or two years. Some readings can give information that focuses years ahead on one particular subject.

It is the beings in the spirit world who come forth with messages for people. I do not have the ability to call someone up from the spirit world; it is they who come forth to me from spirit, and the channel or linkage is made possible through the close love connection between the being in spirit and the person having a reading.

When a spirit has had a close love connection with a person on the earth plane, the love that both parties share with one another manifests a strong energy, enabling the medium to make a much closer connection than if such love were not present. The love they carry for one another seems at times to override any barriers that could disrupt their connection. Both parties are receptive to communicate with one another. Because they have a love link, the spirit is often anxious to make a strong contact through the medium.

I often tell people that they do not actually need me as a channel, since their loved one in spirit will make contact with them on the earth plane during the sleep state. When we go off to sleep, our soul travels up into the astral plane, and this allows us to be relaxed and go even higher into the subconscious awareness state. At the same time, our loved ones on the other side travel down to connect with our energy and light, and we actually visit with them in the spirit world, conversing with one another; we come back in the morning from the sleep state feeling happy and comforted to know our loved ones in the spirit world are alive and happy. A lot of people remember having a dream about a loved one in the spirit world. They think, however, that this was only a dream and have not realized that they are actually connecting and visiting with their loved ones in the spirit world by travelling up into the astral plane in their sleep state. Many people who have lost loved ones will often recall such a dream not long after the person has passed over.

Most people seek out a medium for guidance, reassurance, and comfort. I am always amazed at how much information the spirit world will give me for a person in such a short time. It is very important, however, for my client to understand all the messages being given to them. I give them ample opportunity to ask questions at the end of a reading, and they may interrupt me at any time during the reading if they require any further explanations or clarification of the information being given to them. I ask spirit to give me information on all areas of their lives. For instance, I will look at their health condition. One lady I saw recently was told she needed to take iron badly, because she was feeling very tired. She told me that she had had a blood test the day before her reading, and her doctor had reported that she was very anemic and needed an intake of iron immediately. Often when the spirit world gives a person some health advice—it may be diet or exercise related—the person feels happy to receive these messages.

I also look at a person's spiritual life, and they are given guidance as to how this pathway is flowing for them. People often want to know about material matters, and we usually cover this area during a reading. One of the main reasons I feel people seek out a medium is to talk about their personal lives and make the vital connection with those in the spirit world who can give them clear guidance and direction in this area. It is, however, always made very clear to my clients that they all have free will, and the spirit world will not make their decisions for them. It is not our job to interfere in other people's relationships.

When a medium does a reading, she or he must, first of all, still the mind, switching off from any outside interferences or noises. As it is the love link between the person and those in spirit that we connect with, we must "tune in" to raise our level of conscious awareness, always in control and always connected to the person we are reading for.

I always start a reading with a prayer in my mind. This enhances the level of protection for me and draws in a much brighter light. I never take my gift for granted and request energy from the higher power so that I can always maintain control. I do not want to link with any wayward spirits who wish to give me information that is in any way mischievous or does not relate to the person for whom I am reading. I ask those in the spirit world who wish to make a positive connection to step forward. And I want them all to know that I am in control of my gifts! I always know that I am in control of the spiritual power given to me because of the strong faith I have in God, and I always sense my spirit guide with and around me, giving me protection.

When I begin a reading, I feel a spiritual teacher step in very close to me and pass on messages of wisdom to my client. It is so rewarding when I see how delighted my client is with the messages given and how in tune the spirit world is with them.

I have met some people who call themselves mediums but who do not exercise any control. They will often tell me that they are linking with people who reside in a much higher vibration that those in the spiritual planes. They will tell me that they cannot even tape their readings, as the energy vibration is too powerful! When this happens, it seems to me that they are not in control of their psychic powers and are in fact allowing their egos to drive them along. On several occasions I have had other psychics phone me regarding a murder case. They tell me they have been given, psychically, the name of the person who committed the crime and give me other details. I very quickly tell them to call the police and give them the details, so that they can investigate the information given. If they do not bother to call the police, it seems to me that mischievous spirits may be at work.

To reach the spirit world, I travel upwards in vibrational level, and the people in the spirit world come down to connect with my energy. My spirit guides help me to make the transition upwards to link with spirit as they come down to connect with my energy. It takes a lot of energy to make this connection, and I can feel quite drained after a reading. Also, the spirit will be examining me to see if they feel comfortable with the way I will be interpreting their messages to their loved ones.

Of course, sometimes people communicate from the other side who have had a strained relationship with the person on the earth plane. This communication may be for the purpose of putting things right between them, so that both parties can continue to grow and get on with their lives.

The word *reading* describes mediumship sessions aptly, because I am being given information from spirit about a person, both past and present, and it is like reading chapters in this person's book of life. We all have a book of life, and some books you just can't put down. Everyone's life is interesting, often rewarding, and almost always challenging. I may not see a person for five years, but as soon as I greet them at the door, I often see their book of life immediately opened in front of my eyes, showing and telling me about them; sometimes they will comment that a certain message is exactly the same as one given to them five years ago. The medium is only given information that is relevant to the person seeking counsel, and we are given permission to tune into that person's life at that particular time, by the person requesting the reading.

Our job is to give upliftment, reassurance, and guidance, always linking to the positive energies of life. We must never tell a person what to do, as we must let free will be their guide. It helps when the medium's life is in harmony and balance. This allows us to work with an even vibration and steadiness. We must lead by example!

If a medium misuses their God-given gift, then I believe the gift will be taken from them, or in some way their life will be affected. The law of cause and effect is at work. We must always use our gifts wisely. For example, if a person asks me when spirit thinks they will pass, or asks about someone else, I always say, "It is in God's hands." And it is. Only God knows how long we are to live in this life. Some people on the earth plane have a premonition about the age they think they themselves will pass. Sometimes this is the case, while at other times this premonition actually relates to someone else close to them. I have had young people tell me they do not think they will make twenty-five years . of age, and I have never yet thought they were right. So that idea is dispelled very quickly. The mind is a powerful tool, and if we believe something deeply in our minds, then we can actually bring that event to pass.

When a person is ill, I question whether it is right or not to tell them their illness is terminal, or to put a timing on their lives on the earth plane. Sometimes I wonder if it is like pointing the bone at someone, or in other words, telling them to tell their minds, "It's time to give up."

When a person communicates with me from the spirit world, they will, in most cases, tell me how they passed, whether it be from a heart attack, cancer, an illness, or an accident, or if they have left the earth plane suddenly. Sometimes they will tell me, "I didn't even have time to say good-bye or pack my bag"—not that they need a suitcase or any material objects with them in the spirit world. Thus it may also be helpful to people in spirit when a medium makes a link with them, and they may express their deep appreciation.

Sometimes the person in spirit is distressed or disoriented. Talking with them may give them reassurance and guidance if they feel lost or have fear around them. I often will feel spirits' emotional ache of being separated from their loved on the earth plane. Some spirits do not recognize that they have actually died and still think they are living on the earth plane. They may still be residing as spirits in the home they once lived in; some people would call them ghosts. They wander around aimlessly, and these spirits are called lost souls. Many circles meet weekly under the control of a medium for the purpose of rescuing these lost souls and for helping to send them towards the light and on their way to their new, true place of residence in the spirit world.

Many times, the love generated from the client helps the spirit to settle into its new surroundings so much more easily, and this conscious linking can help direct them towards the light if they have not yet accepted their passing, or as in some cases, they do not realize they have passed to a higher dimension and are still earthbound.

People never lose their personalities when they go to spirit. They are exactly the same, except they have no need for their overcoat or their shell. We leave the flesh behind, and it is just our spirit that goes on. When I see people in spirit, they manifest themselves to me just as they looked here on the earth plane, so that I can get a clear visual picture and description for their loved ones.

Sometimes I have to coax spirit to come forward, perhaps saying, "It's okay, love, you can do it. Just step forward and speak to me; don't feel anxious. I will try and lift my energy higher for you, to make this communication easier." Often they will wait a few moments, until the energy is at a comfortable level, and then begin to communicate with their loved one. Some are overanxious to communicate, and some actually take my breath away, especially if they passed with a lung condition or respiratory problem.

I try to maintain a comfortable energy level in the surroundings to help the client feel relaxed. Usually I sit them down in my readings room with some soothing music and leave them on their own for a few moments. When I return to the room, I find they have calmed down and are feeling more at ease.

Most people have been rushing before they reach my door, and I feel it is healing for them to take this special time out to slow themselves down to communicate with the spirit world. This also helps those in the spirit world to come closer. The energy in my room seems to build up with a residue of healing from the spirit world that helps both myself and the client during readings.

It takes me only a few moments to tune in or switch in with the loved ones in the spirit world. I raise my vibrational level by allowing the God light to enter the top of my head, through my crown chakra area. It has taken me many years to try and perfect the art of communication with the spirit world. I have been tested at times with difficult connections but fortunately have always won through. I may have been on the telephone or doing the dishes before a person arrives to see me for a reading. This does not alter the flow of my communication or energy with the spirit world once a connection is made. Once I stop, relax, and tune in, sitting down quietly and stilling my mind, I feel my head lighten, and, after saying my opening prayer, it all seems to flow naturally. For years while I was developing, it was not so easy, and I felt I was tested a lot by the spirit world in really having to raise my energy levels and push for answers from the spirit world to enable me to give proof and information to those people visiting me.

Once a connection has been made, spirit communicates with me just as though we are good friends having a friendly chat. They may show me how their general health condition was at certain times of their life on the earth plane. Others do not wish to discuss their illness. They may tell me how they passed, but they are really more interested in giving me information for their loved ones on the earth plane.

Spirit may also guide me to a health condition of their loved one on the earth plane, so that they may offer some advice. I always make it perfectly clear that I am not a doctor, that I do not diagnose, but that it is important to have a balance between orthodox medicine and alternative remedies.

People often confirm, after being given advice on a health condition from spirit, that they have just had a visit to a doctor, or an x-ray, and received the same diagnosis. This confirmation is always good for both the client and the medium.

The person in spirit usually tries to help their loved ones on earth to accept their passing and to heal their grief. Both parties find it important to reassure one another that they are reaching a form of acceptance of being parted from one another, so that they each may follow their new-found pathways.

Most mediums are also healers or can act as channels for healing energy, so when a person comes for a reading, they receive healing. They may not be aware of this at first, but feel the upliftment from this healing in the days and months ahead. The healing given to them by spirit in the presence of the medium can be on the emotional level, or the physical, or both can occur at the same time. I have had people tell me that they feel as though a hand has reached inside of them, inside their chest area, and taken away the emotional pain and anguish they have been feeling. Some report feeling as though a great weight were lifted from their shoulders, even while waiting for me in my waiting room prior to a reading.

In fact, spirit is busy working for them all the time. Our guardian angels are always hard at work on our behalf, and it is true that if you pray deeply and sincerely enough for something very important in your life, then your prayers will undoubtedly be answered. "Ask and you shall receive."

I work with love and light in my heart, given to me by God, and I always enjoy working in my own surroundings, but it is not necessary to have perfect conditions in which to work. The gift of mediumship travels with us everywhere we go, and mediums must often work in conditions that are not perfect. Sometimes the surroundings have been quite noisy and disruptive, but the spirit world has never let me down and has always had messages awaiting people.

In order to use their gift properly for the highest good, a medium should always strive to be helpful, and to give people peace of mind, encouragement, and proof that their loved ones in the spirit world are safe and well, happy and at peace, in the new home in the spiritual plane. Bereaved parents need reassuring that babies and children are always met in the spirit world and nurtured along the way. Even so, most parents grieve always for their child; they tend never to get over the loss of a loved one, but learn to live with it. They say the worst thing that can happen to a parent in life is to lose a child, no matter what age, for then we can no longer go into the next room to give them a hug. Parents feel the physical loss of a child so greatly, and besides, the spiritual and emotional link leaves us with part of our heart leaving the earth plane with our loved one.

I encourage parents and all my clients always to think of spirit as being around us, near to us. We can call in our loved ones; they draw near as we think their name or call them to mind. We may not be aware of their presence, but they will be with us, nonetheless, trying to comfort us and give us reassurance that they are, in fact, now on their higher plane.

We all have spiritual guides and helpers assigned to us. It is my band of guides and helpers who do the clearing for me. They are busy at work uplifting the energy around me while I am working, and by doing so, they try to remove the feeling of grief and sadness that may surround the people I work with.

A person may be carrying some baggage from the past (for want of a better word) around with them, and during our time together, a lot of this unwanted baggage will be cleared away from them.

I also have people visit me who have unwanted spirits walking with them, unbeknownst to them. These unwanted spirits may be from a lower astral level and have attached themselves in a sense to the person. By being with a medium, they may be cleared away from the person and sent on their way. Unfortunately, the person who has had the unwanted spirit clinging to them may have felt ill, sad, or had a feeling of anxiousness for some time and was not aware of the cause. To prevent this from happening, we must ask for daily protection from the highest source.

Sometimes people have a lot of personal pain around them. Conditions can just as often be vibrant and extremely happy around a person, but when conditions are low, then the spirit world has to work overtime, in fact putting forth quite a tremendous effort in order to lift that person's energy and vibration and help them. In this way, when I work with spirit, they are "clearing" all the time for me, that is, helping to clear away the dark or heavy fog of pain and grief and make way for the light of healing and truth.

Messages given to me from the spirit world are often quite clear and provided in the most simplistic form. The simple, straightforward character of most messages from spirit has helped me realize that simplicity is indeed a key to successful living. Our pathways in life should be unstructured, clear, simple, and uncomplicated. Simplicity is the key to opening new doors in all our lives. My conversations with the spirit world are as simple as you or I having a conversation or chat with a friend. As I talk to my client, the person in the spirit world gives me messages for that person. The person speaking from spirit is in tune with what is happening in that particular person's life at that time, and they make suggestions or give insights accordingly. I always ask to see or be given helpful information on a person's health condition, their material life, their spiritual life, and their personal life. These four categories cover a lot of information from spirit for any one person.

If you come to a medium, then you have acknowledged, in some way, the life hereafter. Even if a person says to me, "I do not believe in life after death; I am very skeptical," then I say, "It is right to question; it is healthy to ask questions. How else can we learn, if we do not question?"

However, if a person is totally skeptical and will not open up their heart to be receptive to spirit, that can sometimes shut a medium down or prevent a linkage with spirit from taking place. Without faith and belief, and the contribution of positive energy, the negativity flowing to the medium from such a person may even prevent the medium from being able to make a contact. Again, it is the love link the medium works within, and the spirit world will protect the medium and not allow them to be exploited.

I love it, though, when the odd person has told me, "I do not believe in this sort of thing," or "It's a bit of hocus-pocus to me, this thought of ghosts, or the very thought of going on to another life." Still, for some reason or another, that person has been directed to the medium, and I have found in many cases that the person becomes speechless when the spirit world gives them messages about themselves and their lives that no one else could possibly know. I say in my mind to my spiritual guides, "Let's knock their socks off; let them leave here without any doubt of the life hereafter."

Often, before a person comes to a medium for a reading, those in the spirit world have prompted them to come along, so that they may receive a message of guidance, or encouragement, or reassurance that, yes, the client is on the right path; also, the loved one in spirit just wants them to know that they are doing very well.

When helping people we must go into this work with the right attitude, and with love in our hearts. This work is very sensitive and also very confidential. It is good that I seldom remember information about a person after I have read for them, unless it is something very tragic, which may jog my memory.

I always explain to a person when they come for a reading that it helps me to concentrate by closing my eyes from time to time, and that I always get a faraway look in my eyes. This occurs while I am focusing, concentrating, and raising my level of conscious awareness. It takes a lot of energy for mediums to lift themselves up to the higher communicational level. After an hour with one person, I find it is time to come back to the physical and be grounded again. I explain to people that while reading, I could get up and answer the door, but I would still be receiving messages. If an interruption occurs, the person in the spirit world communicating with me may just say, "We will wait for a moment," until I am ready again. Thankfully, I do not allow too many interruptions while working. I feel it is very important to utilize spirit time. Spirit comes forth for these special occasions, and we must treasure our communication time and not take any of it for granted.

Frequently, the loved one in the spirit world will visit me prior to a reading and then be waiting for the connection. This happens when the connection is particularly strong and the love link is powerful. The spirit world always knows prior to your visit that you are coming. In fact, more often than not, they may prompt you to pick up the telephone and make the appointment.

Two conversations are going on at once during a reading, as I am talking to my client and the spirit world at the same time. The clairaudient aspect involves vibrations received by the medium through the subconscious mind. It is as though I have a typewriter printing out information across my mind. I do not hear the voices in my ear, and yet I hear the tone in which they speak, whether it is soft or loud, or in an accent.

Clairvoyantly, the spirits manifest themselves to me as they appeared on the earth plane. They may communicate how they were dressed or looked before they left the earth plane. I've seen men in their hospital pajamas, apologizing to me and reaching for a dressing gown. I am always thankful that the people in spirit seem to have taken their sense of humor over with them, and we do usually have a lot of laughter while visiting with them. This also raises the energy levels around us, or shall I say, it brings up the vibrational levels, and the experience becomes not only touching but very rewarding for all parties concerned.

I always ask spirit to give me names, especially the name of the person I am communicating with, a family name, a surname, or a maiden name. If I am given common names, then I ask spirit for a description of the person named. This helps identify who is being spoken about, especially if my client knows two people who have the same name.

Also, it is quite common for a loved one in the spirit world to mention their funeral. In spirit they may refer to it as their celebration or send-off, as they are going to a much higher dimension. The loved one will describe who was at their funeral, or remark about the music played. It is something I do not dwell upon, but they often like to thank the person who made the arrangements for a lovely and loving gathering of family and friends. It is sometimes overwhelming for a spirit when they have passed over suddenly without saying good-bye to family and friends, when all of a sudden they see from the spirit world a great gathering of family and friends at their funeral service.

Some of these spirits may never have considered that there was a life after death, and they may not even know where they are! They are overwhelmed because of the love they are receiving from those gathered at their funeral service. These people, and their collective love, help the spirit reach a higher dimension.

Some spirits will sit in on their own funeral service quite comfortably. They may describe the music that was played at their service or what key people were wearing who attended the service.

I have had people tell me that they have seen the spirit happily standing next to the coffin during the service. One young Maori man, who was at his grandmother's funeral, told me he heard his name being called from the back of the church. He turned around and saw his grandmother standing there. He got quite a fright, as she called his name again and waved to him. He saw her as clear as a bell. She disappeared after a few moments. He turned back and saw the coffin sitting at the front of the altar. He told me, "I knew she wasn't really dead."

If someone is holding on to a person's ashes, the spirit person may tell me to tell them just where they would like them released, and in nine out of ten cases, that is exactly where the person holding the ashes had thought to scatter them.

I believe that families regroup again in the spirit world before coming back to the earth plane, especially if the love link is strong. Passage of time in spirit is just a flash of the eyelid, compared to our concept of time on the earth plane.

But it is not as though the "time" spent in spirit between times on earth passes idly by. I see people playing musical instruments in the spirit world, or working and playing with the spirit children, or sitting in the garden, making cups of tea or coffee, or baking—all sorts of different situations. Spirit often will be found doing a job they did on the earth plane, and they might tell me how they worked, before they passed over. If a person was physically disabled, maybe in a wheelchair at some stage in their life, then they may appear that way during a reading, to enable me to identify them to their loved ones.

Animals also appear to me from spirit. Family pets may show themselves to me and communicate by sitting at their loved ones' feet. Many times the family pet was alive for many years and became part of the family. Pets can be just like our children. We can transmit so much love to them, and we all know how loving and loyal our pets can be. This loyalty seems to stay with them, as their spirit continues to walk through life with you. They are also loved in the spirit world and are cared for with much tenderness by the guardian angels.

Every good medium looks for proof and as much helpful information as they can possibly give a person while reading for them. If a person on the earth plane is wearing a lot of jewelry, you can almost guarantee the person in the spirit world will point out to me a ring or piece of jewelry. Often I see them pointing and telling me, "I gave him that watch," or "She's wearing my broach." Also, they may describe jewelry that the person isn't wearing on this day, and this is a good proof, to be able to tell a person what they have at home in their jewelry box.

At times, the person in spirit will describe a home familiar to the client. I've been in more homes than a realtor, I'm sure—that is, homes in my mind, as I am shown around by spirit. I've seen people doing renovations, alterations, building new homes, painting the house, and decorating with furniture and different color schemes. I find it all very interesting.

I have even had people think that I have driven past their homes and peeked through the windows, as the descriptions I relate to them are so accurate. Of course, this is never the case, and never would be. How would we find the time? Besides, some of these descriptions are of homes on the other side of the world, such as a family member's home in England, or elsewhere. One day I was reading for a lady and was looking around her home in my mind, when I heard her say to me telepathically, "Get out of my house!" She was a very private person, and only invited guests were allowed in! As I apologized to her, she blushed and said, "You must have read my thoughts."

It is of the utmost importance that a medium maintain a positive attitude and look after their physical body, as this work can be physically draining. It is most important to have a balanced diet, and to exercise on a regular basis, as this work requires a lot of sitting. If we allow negative thoughts to come through, then our inner lights will be dimmed and our energy levels lowered. So, I have learned always to focus on a bright light above my head, ready to light up like a bulb and shed light all around. I also encourage everyone to do the same, as this will brighten any situation.

Mediumship offers faith to a great many. Being touched by the spiritual experience of a reading can change people's lives, open new doors within them that may have been shut tight for many years, or perhaps open doors that people have been afraid to open. The encouragement and upliftment received may link a person with their chosen pathway, the spiritual pathway. If you have had a touching experience by linking with the spirit world, then I am sure you will believe forever in the eternal life of the soul. Not only will this knowledge and belief help you in this lifetime, but also in your next life, the life hereafter.

We mediums experience the rewards and wonderful satisfaction of helping humanity when we work with love in our hearts, a love given to us from a higher dimension, which enables us to connect people with loved ones in the spirit world.

CHAPTER FIVE

How Spirit Works
to Connect with Us

WHILE COMMUNICATING with the spirit world, I have had some interesting and pre-orchestrated occurrences take place, sometimes when working in front of large groups of people, giving out individual messages, and other times during private sessions.

For instance, a loved one from the spirit world may be waiting to connect and feeling very anxious to make that connection. Sometimes, because of this anxiousness, the spirit misses cues, as I call it, and steps into someone else's reading. When this happens, I have to ask the spirit to wait for the right connection.

Then I have had days of working where the same name of a spirit person reoccurs for three readings in a row. Having the confidence to give out the same name to three consecutive clients is testing, especially when you question spirit in your mind and ask, "Are you sure that's your name? It's the same name as the person before you." However, I have learned from experience to trust and pass that name on anyway. I never hesitate to do so now, and in nine out of ten cases it will be the correct name.

This unexplained phenomenon has occurred frequently enough to make me wonder whether the Davids queue up one day and the Barbaras on another day to make contact through the medium.

Spirit can work in unusual ways. People come for various reasons and are given information that appears totally insignificant at that time. Then, sometimes hours or days later, the new information becomes a reality when they meet a person or experience an event that has been given to them during the course of a reading. Only then does the message make sense.

I remember asking a lady one day, "Do you know a George?"

"No," she replied.

"Well," I said, "spirit is telling me about a George; he is tall with fair hair and has a moustache; he drives a red sports car."

"I cannot think who that would be," she said.

The spirit message continued, "Well, you soon will."

When she went back to work that afternoon, a gentleman by the name of George who was tall, with blond hair and a moustache, drove up to her office in a red sports car. She was a realtor, and he wanted her to show him some properties. She telephoned me that very afternoon to confirm the message she had been given from spirit, and that she had met the man named George.

Another lady in her early sixties, who had been living by herself for some time came for a private reading. I asked her, "Do you know who Charlie is?"

"I wouldn't have a clue," she replied.

Her grandfather, giving me the message for her from spirit, laughed and said to her, "Well dear, there is a surprise coming your way."

She telephoned me several months later to say she had met a lovely gentleman called Charlie, and they had become great friends.

Some spirits find it difficult to take their turn to communicate through the medium. Sometimes spirit will link with me enough so that I can recognize their presence, but then just stand in the room and not communicate. This tells me they were probably shy or withdrawn when they were on the earth plane. At other times, two or three spirits will jostle for my attention and I will have to say to them, "Bless you all for coming to make a communication, but one at a time, please."

If a client has lost someone very close to them, then the loved one in the spirit world will come in close and make contact quickly.

Sometimes I am shown symbols to interpret, particularly when the spirit is not getting my complete attention or when I do not hear a name of a person clearly.

I remember being shown a symbol for a lady I was reading for who had a father in the spirit world. He was communicating well with me but was unable to give me his name. All of a sudden during the reading he showed me a picture of William Tell with his bow and arrow about to shoot the apple from the young boy's head. "Now what is he trying to tell me?" I wondered. "Does his daughter participate in archery?" But no, I realized that he was trying to tell me that his name was William. His daughter and I laughed about the clever way in which he had proceeded to get his message across.

As I am only given a few symbols from time to time to work with, I interpret them as they are given to me. Sometimes the spirit world makes me work a little harder to define these symbols, but it is usually within a few moments that I am able to see a clear picture of what they mean.

I find myself prompting the spirit world to talk with me as clearly as they possibly can, rather than have me work with too many symbols. I really want to be spoiled and work with them as directly and clearly as I possibly can. I ask my spiritual guides not to give me too many symbols and ask to be given details that are clearly distinguishable between myself and the client.

Everyone involved in this work has a different personality and different aptitudes, and in most cases this reflects in their method of working and communicating with the spirit world. My spiritual guides have determined the most appropriate way for me to work, which is by using only my clairvoyant and clairaudient gifts, and without the need of any other material item. I aim for accuracy and to give as much proof of the life hereafter as I can.

When I do get symbols given to me, I believe my spiritual guidance is providing them to assist me in interpreting an unusual name or in getting a message clearly for my client. However, I continually ask spirit to talk to me directly rather than in symbols. But some people in spirit are better verbal communicators than others, depending on how well they were able to communicate when they were on the earth plane, so that might account for some of the variations in communication styles.

I remember seeing a lady who had a daughter on the earth plane who was very close to her. As I tuned in for this girl's name, I saw her mother dressed in red, a dress very similar to the one Scarlet O'Hara wore in *Gone with the Wind*. This seemed a little unusual to me, but I might not have mentioned it to her if the vision had not been so strong. However, I passed the message on, saying that I could see the mother dressed like Scarlet O'Hara. "Oh," she remarked, "I can relate to that message, Jenny; we named our daughter Tara, after the name of the house in *Gone with the Wind*.

Flowers are often shown to me as symbols by the spirit world. In fact, flowers are blessings from the spirit world. The colors of flowers can be significant for an individual. Spirit will often give me the name of a particular flower or plant that has been planted in their memory. I have different interpretations of colors, and roses of different colors are always particularly significant to me. For example, the color pink is for love, gold is for success, yellow is for friendship, white is for blessings, red for celebration and romance, and mauve for change and spiritual growth. The colors of blues and greens are for healing and improved health.

I often will see one of the seven colors of the rainbow for a person during a reading. The particular color is a healing color and shown to me with a person's aura. I also may ask that a person choose their own rainbow color and visualize themselves draped in that color for the day, especially when they feel their energies are low.

Spirit will often show me a gold cross being placed around a person's neck, and my interpretation of this is that spirit is offering this person a spiritual blessing. It is my belief that religion is universal and that one's faith comes from the heart and the soul, for that is where our personal place of worship can be found.

I have also met and read for many people who belong to genealogy societies, who know all their family trees and their ancestor's names. I find this very helpful, particularly when a great-great-grandmother steps forward from the other side to make a communication. It is so nice for the spirit when they can be identified immediately by a family member.

It is marvelous to experience the wonderful sense of humor that people have and take with them to the spirit world. I may be reading for a person when a connection of their's in the spirit world will tell me that they have a grumpy family member around them at the moment. Sometimes it is not the message that is so funny, but the way it is told to me. Often the grumpiness is health- or stress-related, and the spirit will give some guidance for that person.

I saw a gentleman in his mid-forties, not long after his father had passed over. His dad wasted no time in telling me that they were very close. He went on to tell me how he had remarried during his life on earth and that he had not been happy with his new wife. He felt she had married him for his money and wanted to spend it all.

His son did not get on with his stepmother either. I was trying to be diplomatic while passing on these messages. As the father kept talking to me I could hardly hear him at all, as he was laughing so hard! "Please tell me what is so funny," I asked him.

He went on to tell me that he had hidden ten thousand dollars in the garden for his son, which he told his son about only days before he passed over. "I had to hide the money," he told me. "I did not want my wife to get her hands on it." His son had gone to his property while the stepmother was out and dug up the money, which was where his father had said it would be.

Unbeknownst to the son, the stepmother must have had an inkling that there was some money buried on the property. When the son went to collect some of his father's personal belongings that had been bequeathed to him, he saw his stepmother outside with a spade, digging up what seemed like the whole yard.

"I know it's here somewhere," she told him.

The stepson asked her, "What is here? What are you looking for?"

"The money, of course," she replied. "I know he's buried it here somewhere. He always tried to hide the money from me."

The stepson smiled as he walked away. His father told me he would dine out on this for eternity. "She never picked a spade up in her life before, and she certainly couldn't stand to garden," he said, as his laughter drifted into the distance.

I must admit it was rather funny under the circumstances. I knew that the stepmother was well provided for, so I felt I could afford to laugh with them.

Not only do people take their lovely personalities with them, but they are still able to bring people joy on the earth plane with their sense of humor. Laughter is one of the best medicines for us all. Laughter brings healing and changes tears of sadness to joy and upliftment. Laughter is music to warm the soul. Laughter makes the sun shine.

I am often given songs during a reading. Songs can serve to prompt me to hear the names of spirit people, or they may be tunes that were significant to both parties when they were together on the earth plane. Spirit may tell me, "We sang that song just before I passed over."

I remember giving a lady a message during a meeting; however, I could not hear her name clearly in my mind. Then I saw in my mind what looked like Florence Nightingale, in her nurse's uniform and red cross band on her arm. I said to the lady, "I'm getting the name Florence."

"Yes," she said, "that is my name."

"Your sister in the spirit world is telling me you are a nurse."

"Yes, that is correct," she said.

"Well, your sister is telling me that you are a humanitarian nurse and not only help to heal the sick, but also you help to nurse those souls who need extra nurturing and caring." What a delightful way of giving me a name, I thought to myself.

Sometimes spirit communicates through me via body language, facial expressions, or gestures, as well as words. Often a client will say, "My mother always used to say that to me when she was alive," or, "You are holding your hands together just how Dad used to," or, "Your facial expression is exactly like the expression my son used to have on his face."

Sometimes a spirit person will wink at me, and I do my best to pass this wink on. The client will nearly always glow with a warm smile or just burst out laughing, as this may have been a familiar habit of their loved one. I always look and ask spirit for significant signs such as facial expressions, bodily injuries, or any piece of information that may be relevant for the person receiving a reading as proof of the life hereafter. The clearest proofs tend to be names and descriptions of loved ones in the spirit world and messages that give information that no one else could possibly have known about.

As I mentioned before, only occasionally do I see a client who will sit in their chair and be switched off from me completely, or show a tremendous amount of negativity. This generally stems from the sadness of their particular circumstances at that time. It can be difficult to work with a person who has closed themselves off in this way. I find that I become drained both mentally and physically and can be very tired after this happens; thankfully the client nearly always leaves with a smile on their face and hope in their heart.

If a person comes to me with a genuine purpose of need, then the messages tend to be very clear. I find that those who come with an open heart and receptive to spirit help make the communication a lot stronger.

I always explain to people that I do not want them to offer me any information about their lives either before or during the reading. I do not make any personal assumptions about people; I rely totally on the information being given to me from the spirit world. I might ask them from time to time that if they understand a message, they should confirm with a yes or no. I have read for people who do not utter one word during their reading, and the only feedback I have had is when they phone for another appointment in six months' time and tell me then that the messages they had received had all fallen into place. Only then do I learn whether the reading contained any proof or help for the client.

I usually explain to my client before a reading that it helps to hear their voice during the reading, not to offer me any information about themselves, but to hear their voice, as this spoken vibration helps draw their love link in closer from the other side. I do encourage my client to give me a yes or no from time to time, as their link in the spirit world will draw in a lot closer at hearing the sound of their voice. In reminding them not to offer up any information about themselves, I tell them that I rely totally on what the spirit world is telling me and bringing through for them. If they have any questions during the reading or do not understand any information, then it is their right to question. However, in many instances their questions are answered before they have the chance to ask!

Travel is a subject that comes up frequently, and it is always interesting when I see a vision of a person travelling to a different destination than where they had planned. One such case was a lady by the name of Velda, who had booked her airfares to go to Perth in Australia.

"Oh no," I said, "You are not going to Perth, my dear; you are going to Canada for a holiday. I can see the Canadian flag flying above your head."

She laughed and assured me that she was going off to Perth. "My tickets are booked and paid for," she told me. Two months later Velda phoned me to say her trip had been cancelled to go to Perth, and the travel group had decided to go to Canada instead. Velda was surprised but happy with this outcome.

Once I saw a large leopard as a symbol given for a lady client. The leopard flashed at me as large as life out of the corner of my eye while I was reading for her. "Why on earth would I see a leopard?" I thought to myself. "This cannot be the family pet, surely!" The lady said, "Thank you Jenny. I have been wondering whether I should take this trip or not. My husband has been planning for months to go on a safari, and before I came to see you today I asked the spirit world to give me a sign of an animal to confirm if I was meant to go."

When I am working in front of large groups of people, giving out clairvoyant messages to individuals, I call this platform work. Sometimes when doing platform work, I will be asked to stand on a stage in front of an audience. Perhaps this is where the name platform originated. It is very exciting working in front of large groups of people. I love the vibrational energy and atmosphere that is generated from a large gathering of people.

Doing platform work in front of large audiences takes a great deal of energy and concentration, largely due to the great number of spirit connections to be made.

It usually takes a few days to build myself up for the event, and I keep a low profile until after the meeting is over. I need all the energy I can generate for such occasions, so I refrain from private readings for several days prior, thus building up my own spiritual energy levels.

I always feel nervous prior to large public meetings, as all the spiritual connections must be provided as clearly and concisely as possible. I never know how many people will attend the meetings, nor who will attend. Perhaps a case of nerves is a sign of being consciously concerned about my work. It certainly never allows me to become complacent.

I always remind myself prior to public meetings that I am only the channel chosen to relay the messages from the spirit world to their loved ones here on the earth plane, and this generally helps me immensely in getting through any cases of nerves.

At one such public meeting, a young man came in to me very closely from the spirit world. He had waited until near the end of the meeting, as other spirits had been flooding in to make their communications with loved ones in the audience. This young man stepped forward very strongly and announced his name to me as Tony. He told me he was looking for his dad in the audience, a man by the name of Anthony. His dad quickly raised his arm, claiming the name. Tony told me he was christened Anthony, but everyone called him Tony. I could see that he was a tall, dark-haired, very handsome young man with a lovely personality. During his link with me, I kept holding my head with my fist on top of my forehead. I could not understand this.

I said to his father, "Anthony, I cannot deliver this message to you from your son unless I have my hand on my forehead." Tony whispered to me in spirit, "Dad knows why; Dad knows why."

Tony then gave me details about two friends, Tim and Peter, who had travelled a lot with him. His father acknowledged this and went on to tell me and the audience that Tony had been blown up in an accident, and the only physical part of his body that had been left was his head. Tony had linked with me from the spirit world as being physically normal, but to get his message across he needed to show me the feeling of holding his head. His father was a very spiritual man himself, and the connection with Tony this evening helped to heal the emotional effects of his passing.

At another public meeting, I pointed to a young man at the back of the hall. His father in the spirit world gave him a message, which the son accepted; the father went on to say, with a big smile on his face, that he had a large dog around him.

"He tells me you have an Alsatian dog."

"Yes, that's correct," the young man called out from the back of the hall.

It was a warm evening, and all the doors were open in the hall. As this message was delivered, right on cue, and in front of everyone in the hall, a large Alsatian dog walked in and sat right at this young man's feet, much to all our amusement.

When I am reading for a person in an audience, I often see a light around them, sometimes just a blue light flashing above their head, but if a strong message is being delivered, I will see the person light up with a golden light around them.

Another man rushed in to me from spirit during a public meeting, telling me he did not want to miss out and that he had just recently passed with a heart attack. "I'm Irish," he told me.

"I can hear that, love, by your accent," I told him.

He gave me his name, and I saw him clearly. He told me his son and daughter-in-law were in the audience, and he was anxious to make contact with them. Sadly, they did not claim the message until after the meeting. The Irish man's son was too shy, and he said to me later that he knew that it was his dad but felt a little shy to claim the message, and I had not pointed to him. The medium and spirit work very hard to make this communication, and people at these meetings must be willing to participate. Fortunately for this gentleman, he was able to make another contact with his dad during a private reading.

One time, a new spiritual group was starting up, and one of our local/international mediums, Maureen Chapman, phoned me and asked if I would take the meeting for this new group. Yes, I replied, thinking this would start me off again doing public work, and expecting that the group would be very small.

When I arrived, the hall was packed with people; many were standing at the back of the hall. My knees started to tremble a bit; before the meeting started, I seemed to have to take numerous trips to the bathroom. In situations like this, I have to give myself a good talking to and remember that I am just the channel working for the spirit world, and yes, I have come to work.

As I stood in front of this audience, spirit asked me to take the audience through a guided meditation. I felt comfortable with this, although in situations where there are larger groups gathered, I prefer to take them on a simple, loving, and healing journey where we travel together and everyone feels safe, protected, and secure with their surroundings—a short meditation that would fill people's hearts with hope and joy, giving them a new sense of inner peace and spiritual renewal.

As I stood guiding this meditation, you could have dropped a pin and everyone would have heard it. The evening went on as I gave a talk about people believing in themselves and following through with their dreams and aspirations in life. After all, God loves a dreamer.

Soon it was time for me to do clairvoyance. Public clairvoyance can be nerve-wracking to begin with, as mediums do not rehearse beforehand; we have to wait to see who steps forward from the spirit world to give out the messages. I began to feel a queue of people lining up in the spirit world to give messages.

I spoke for a moment to the audience regarding clairvoyance, asking people to claim messages when they were given to them. Some people may feel shy or embarrassed to claim a message, and it is difficult for the people in the spirit world, who have fought so hard to come through, when this occurs. It can make the spirit very sad when a communication is not made.

I began tuning in and was very quickly directed to an old gentleman at the side of the hall. He was a small man, neatly dressed in a pale blue pullover and grey trousers. His face looked to me as though he had suffered considerable emotional pain. I pointed to the gentleman as he looked around to see who I was going to give a message to. "Me?" he said.

"Yes, you, my dear," I said. "I have a lady in the spirit world who wishes to speak with you. She tells me she is your wife, whom you nursed for many years before she passed over. She was ever so grateful to you for your loving and caring attention."

Before the message could continue, the old man stood up, astounded, tears rolling down his face, and said, "Oh, my God, I have been waiting to hear from her for years." The audience chuckled as he called out, "How on earth do you know these things?" He went on to say, "I was told by a friend to come tonight, that I might receive a message. You do not know what you have done for me; thank you." His message flowed on, and I felt very humble to be the channel delivering such a message.

This same gentleman queued up to thank me at the end of the evening, and we had a big hug together. As he stood holding a cup of tea, his hands shaking, I told him he too was intuitive, and perhaps one day I would call around and we would read tea cup leaves together! He thought this suggestion was great and said to call in anytime.

The messages flowed on, and I announced to the audience that I had a Mavis in spirit; did anyone know a Mavis in the spirit world, down the back of the hall? There was no response, so I decided to move on. "I'm sorry, Mavis," I said to her. "No one is claiming you."

Just then a young man put his hand up and said he knew an Avis in the spirit world. "Sorry, love," I replied, "this lady tells me her name is Mavis." As I looked again into the hall, I saw a lady with a light around her, and she raised her hand. Mavis was my aunty she told me. Mavis took no time in telling her niece that she was moving house.

"You have had strong words with your son," she tells me, "and you have now directed him onto the right pathway."

"Yes," she replied. "That is true."

"Well, my dear, your Aunty Mavis says not to feel guilty about it, as he needed this good talking to." She smiled for the first time since I began relaying her message to her.

The lady called out, "Where am I going?" As she did so, Mavis whispered to me, "Australia, of course," which I repeated to her.

"Oh, my goodness," she replied, "I have only been thinking about going to Australia in the last week."

I replied, "They are pretty clever in the spirit world."

The next message I gave was to a lady with her head down, sitting in the back of the hall. "I want to come to the lady wearing the white sweater." She still looked down until her friend sitting beside her tapped her on the shoulder. As she looked up, she blushed. "Does the name John mean anything to you?" I asked.

"Yes," she replied, "my husband and my father."

"Your father is in the spirit world?"

"No," she replied. "He is nearly there."

"Well, my dear, the spirit world tells me it is all in God's hands how long any of us live, but please know that your father John is going to have a safe passage to the spirit world, where he will be loved and protected. Now a message for you: you have been feeling very confused about your pathway of direction, and I have a lady here who tells me her name is Betty."

"Yes," she replied, "my grandmother."

"Well, my dear, your grandmother tells me that you must get moving and put all your ideas into focus. You have been lacking confidence, and now you must move ahead with your business ideas. You are lacking iron and vitamin B complex in your system. Please consider taking these vitamins to alleviate tired-ness and to rebuild your confidence and self-esteem."

The lady called out, "I have been feeling so tired."

Many messages flowed through me as the evening progressed, and I was sad when the time ran out for relaying messages from the spirit world to their loved ones in the audience.

Some messages were simple, and others seemed to hold a strong and profound impact. I really feel it is hard for the medium to judge just what impact the messages bring to individuals, but I knew in my heart that my guides had done their very best to bring positive messages through of upliftment and encouragement. The evening ended with a closing prayer, and I felt very humbled and privileged to be part of an audience that held so much light and love. This evening gave me the confidence and courage to step out again in front of large audiences delivering messages from the spirit world.

As Rob and I drove away from the meeting, I said in my mind, "Thank you, God, for allowing me to be a messenger, and thank you to my spiritual guides; I love you all."

From time to time I have had the opportunity to do platform work before an audience while working in conjunction with a psychic artist. A psychic artist works with images and impressions given to them through their third eye. Our third eye is our psychic eye. As the artist starts to draw or paint, a picture will begin to form very quickly of either a person who has departed to the spirit world or a person's spirit guide.

Some psychic artists also possess the gift of being clairvoyant, enabling them to see the spirit they are drawing quite clearly.

When a medium works with a psychic artist, the medium will give a message to an individual in an audience describing some of the stronger features of the person they are linking with in the spirit world. The psychic artist busily captures this image on canvas, while the medium continues giving out a message.

The psychic also tunes in to the person, and it is alarming how accurate both parties can be, working together. During a meeting with an Australian psychic artist called Marian Ruffin, I remember one message that I relayed to a lady in the audience. Her aunty was talking with me from spirit and giving me a description of herself. Marian had already captured this lady on canvas, and when the lady in the audience saw the picture, she was absolutely thrilled at how accurate the picture was.

She was so impressed that she called around to our home a few days later and showed me a photograph of her aunty, which we both compared with the psychic artist's painting, and I was also excited at the authenticity of this picture. It is good to see the work of a psychic artist proven.

On one occasion I had the delightful opportunity to work with a wonderful psychic artist, and many people came forward to claim their pictures and give confirmation that they recognized the person who had been drawn.

I have read for people who are terminally ill, and I have found that the spirit world always provides the right message in these circumstances. Spirit will give such strong comfort and reassurance, not only to the loved ones who will be left behind on the earth plane, but they will also show people the beautiful place to which they will be going—a place to grow spiritually, where they can rest in peace. I feel privileged and humble to share such messages with these special people.

I once read for a lady just three weeks prior to her passing. She passed very suddenly, and a close friend of hers telephoned me to tell me the sad news, but also to say, "You knew she was going to pass, didn't you, Jenny?"

I said to her, "I had no idea."

Yes, I remembered the lady; she was a beautiful soul. But I was given no indication of her passing.

She said to me, "I listened to my friend's tape, and you said that it was such a great privilege and honor to be spending this time with her. You continually praised her and made her feel very special. She came to me after the reading and said she had not felt so much love around her for such a long time."

The spirit world works through me in ways that I am not even aware of at the time. When receiving feedback from clients, I am so often amazed at how cleverly a message has been coordinated for that person. A message may be given in a way that the person is left to make their own interpretation. The advice and teachings given to clients are often subtly put together and can be far beyond my comprehension at times. It gives me goose bumps when I get feedback from people as to some of the information they have been given, and how this message has been applied to their lives.

Many clients receive messages from the spirit world to give up smoking, as it affects their health. In fact, we do not need spirit to give us such messages, as we can simply tell this to another person. But when spirit tells me that a person will have a shadow on their lung within eighteen months if they do not quit, then I feel it is my humanitarian duty to pass this message on. Dorothy was one such case. She was told to quit before the cigarettes quit her. "A spot will develop on your left lung, Dorothy," was the message from her father in spirit. He had passed with lung cancer.

"Throw those cigarettes away before it is too late."

Sadly, Dorothy did not listen to the advice given to her, and I was to see her eighteen months later, just six weeks prior to her passing. She had a large growth on her left lung which was inoperable, and the cancer was spreading throughout her body. Unfortunately, Dorothy is no longer with her family and friends on the earth plane.

I have met many people who were able to reverse a doctor's diagnosis by caring for themselves and turning to alternative remedies. If it is our time, then we will not be able to reverse any illness we have, but we must make every effort to heal ourselves and really put our heart and soul into this effort. By thinking positively, healing our mind and body, and telling an illness to leave our body immediately, together with regular exercise and healthy eating, we can heal ourselves.

Frequently, a woman will come for a reading, and spirit will tell me she is pregnant. The woman will often deny this and not be aware of it until a few days later, when my phone will ring and she will confirm this news. One lady I had read for over a period of five years said to me, "My husband says I am to stay away from you. Each time I have had a reading during the past three years you've seen me pregnant, and now that we've just had our third child, he says it's time to stop."

I'm not quite sure what he meant.

Many mediums have the ability also to receive communications through the sense of feeling. I often feel pain in a physical sense, experiencing a person's physical state the way it was before their passing. I often ask spirit to step back from me in severe cases, especially if they passed over due to lung problems, as it will take my breath away. In a similar way, if they have choked, I may find myself gulping for breath during a private reading.

I always aim to bring people proof of the life hereafter, and names are wonderful keys to open these doors. One lady said to me after her reading, "I have had many friends come to see you, Jenny, and they have explained to me how you work, but I thought to myself you will not be able to communicate with anyone close to me, as all my close relatives are living on the earth plane. I was surprised that the day before I came to you, I suddenly thought about my Uncle Peter who has been gone for years, and my cousin Alice, who I hardly knew. This was my first experience of a reading, and I found it very fascinating when you were to bring through and name my Uncle Peter and my Cousin Alice. I am now convinced that there is a life when we pass."

Connecting with our loved ones in spirit does not always have to be with a close relative. It can be a lady or gentleman who lived across the street from you when you were a child. It may be the dear old lady from whom you rented a property. Whoever the contact may be, they will always bring you the confirmation, reassurance, and beautiful upliftment you may need at that particular moment.

If a spirit wants to make a communication with a person who is sitting with a medium, they will be guided by a beacon of light that is being projected from the medium and their client. The spirit will draw in close to make this connection with the knowledge that they once knew my client or some members of their family during their lifetime. They may not have been a close love link of my client, but through communicating with the medium, the spirit is ever hopeful that the person receiving their messages will, in turn, pass them on to a loved one on the earth plane on their behalf. The spirit making the connection would be well aware that my client knows the person to whom they seek the message be forwarded.

My interpretation is that the spirit world has a gigantic computer with details of our forward movements. When a person makes an appointment to see me, the spirit world already knows about it or perhaps has set the thought in the person's mind during the sleep state and has actually prearranged this meeting. We gain so many of our ideas and inspirations from the spirit world while in the sleep state. I think the power of suggestion may be at work here. It seems that the people in the spirit world are always looking for ways to contact their loved ones on the earth plane, and they will utilize any opportunity they possibly can to enable a message to be passed on. For example, I may see a mother who has a son living on the earth plane. The son may have a friend in the spirit world. The friend will mention the lady's son, generally naming him, in the hope that his message will filter through and also that his parents get to hear that he is fit and well. Often the spirit will ask, after making this type of connection, that the client please pass their message on to family members. These visits give reassurance to families during their time of grief and healing.

I once read for a lady called Susan, who had a landlady in the spirit world. The landlady, whose name was Dorothy, came through and thanked her for keeping the house she had rented so tidy. She went on to say, "Susan was the best tenant I ever had." Dorothy also told me she passed over with cancer, which had started in her left breast. Susan confirmed this. Dorothy went on to tell me how her house adjoined her rental property. She told me that Susan used to sweep the pathway each day. Susan chuckled and said, "I never thought she even noticed!"

Dorothy said, "I have come to thank my tenant, as when she moved from my house, we missed saying good-bye to one another." Susan was astounded that Dorothy had made her way into her reading to say good-bye to her and to thank her for being such a good tenant.

A spirit will make contact with us when they need to tell us something. When the silver cord has been severed and a spirit has departed from the earth plane very quickly, they may make a communication through a medium to pass on messages, in an attempt to sort out any unfinished business they may have left behind before they departed.

The messages and manner in which spirit communicates, and the amount of comfort, reassurance, humor, and upliftment that spirit continually works to convey to those on earth, always keeps me humble and appreciative of being one assisting vehicle through which some of this work can take place

CHAPTER SIX

When the Silver Cord Is Severed

SOME PEOPLE ASK ME, "Why do you believe in another life, or the life hereafter?" My answer to them is plain and simple: because it has been proven to me over and over again. The spirit world communicates with me every day of my life, continuously bringing through proof of survival. Perhaps we should ask those who do not believe to prove *their* argument.

How sad it can be for those who do not believe in the life hereafter. I always think, what a waste of time it is, coming back down to the earth plane and going through all our ups and downs, our highs and lows, emotional trials, and strengthening times, if it isn't for a real and valid reason.

For years I have wanted to shout from the highest mountain, the highest rooftop, to share this knowledge: Yes, there is a life after we have finished with this one. Already millions and millions of people know this, but, sadly, multitudes of people do not believe this or have not been directed to their awakening of this awareness.

There is another life, one that takes us to a higher dimension—a life that often gives us peace and tranquility, a life that takes away our physical pain and sometimes helps us work through our emotional pain. When a person passes into their next life, they carry with them any emotional pain or problems that were unresolved while in the physical body. The spirit will be given the opportunity to resolve some of their emotional pain and problems. This process is worked through with the spiritual teachers in the spirit world.

When a person arrives in the spirit world, they are shown two books. Each book represents their life on the earth plane. The first book has a detailed record of how that person actually conducted their life while in their physical body. The second book is the master blueprint; this book shows how they were meant to conduct their lives. The spirit is shown the comparison of both books. The spirit may have many lessons pointed out to them. If they have been unkind or cruel to another person on the earth plane, then the spiritual teacher will address these issues with them. This is why it is so important for each of us to make good of each living moment and each breath we take while living on the earth plane. The more we sort out our lives while we are living, the better it is for us in our next life. It is up to each individual to listen to their own guidance and follow their own direction. We are all given free will to make our own decisions. It is so important when making our decisions in life for people not to deviate from a pathway that is well lit for them.

The Buddhist and Hindu religions believe that a person's actions in one lifetime determine his fate in the next lifetime. This is where the word *karma* originates. You may have heard a person say that they feel they are repaying a karmic debt. This is evident when we are put in a situation that we do not enjoy. An example might be a work situation where we feel locked into our occupation and cannot seem to break away from it. Under these circumstances we are usually repaying a karmic debt that has occurred in a previous life time. It may well be that we are indebted to our employer, and once we have succeeded in working hard and repaying this debt by persevering with our job for a period of time, then this will enable us to move on in life. It is as though we are clearing away any blockages from our past.

People often repay karmic debts when working through difficult relationships. Perhaps they have been together in another lifetime with their partner and have come back in this lifetime to resolve any differences before each soul can move on in life comfortably.

I believe we have many lifetimes, and through the process of reincarnation we are given the opportunity for our souls to evolve. They say that we bring forward our fears and anxieties from past lives. Each lifetime gives us the opportunity to resolve some of the fears and anxieties that we have brought forward with us. We are given the opportunity to gain strength from our weaknesses, and sometimes even joy can manifest from painful experiences.

With all the lessons given to us, if we do not learn from them in one lifetime, then we must keep returning to the earth plane until we do. If we conduct our lives in a loving and honest manner, being kind and caring to our fellow man and trying to connect with our higher consciousness, then I believe each time we come back to the earth plane our lessons will be lighter and lighter and our souls will feel freer and freer.

They say we set our own lessons and tests before we return to the earth plane. Many find this hard to believe when they consider the hard path they have chosen. One consolation is that we learn from these lessons and tests, and our future incarnations become easier as each soul becomes more evolved.

We are required by karmic law to make peace with those we have left behind on the earth plane. If we have not treated a person in the right way, we must make amends. Then, in spirit, we must work towards sending love and guidance from the spirit world to help balance the effects of our previous actions.

This other life heals our bodies and our souls, as we do not take our bodies with us to the spirit world; only our souls go on. The soul gains so much healing from passing into the spirit world. They see their whole life flash before them and come to a realization about many issues that they may not have addressed while living on the earth plane. The soul gains a new-found energy in the spirit world. They say that there are hospitals in the spirit world, places of peace and tranquility, where a soul is taken to heal, to regain strength, and to be guided by the spirit teachers. This new-found freedom for the soul brings forward a great surge of healing and upliftment.

Our spiritual pathways are self-chosen. We cannot convince someone else to leap onto their spiritual pathway. Instead, we must quietly lead by example, and when it is their time, they will join us. Many people are spiritual souls without shouting from the rooftops. They act spiritually in every day and in every way, just by being loving and caring souls and supporting humanity. After all, that is really what we all have come back to do—to learn, share, spread light and love, and make our planet a healing center, free of wars, and free of bad vibrations.

When we pass over, or die, as some people describe it, and we have previously decided to be buried, then our bodies, or our physical shells, are like an envelope going into the ground, while our spirit is like a letter that has been posted. We just leave our overcoat behind. We do not need our physical shell any longer. Our spirit is free, not needing the physical body any longer. I believe that it has already been decided as to how much time we live, and how we will pass over. We have free will, but the plan for our passing is not meant to be altered.

It is never the right decision for us to alter our karma, as with people who decide to leave the earth plane and commit suicide. Even writing the word makes me very sad and causes me to shudder!

We are not meant to decide our own fate here on the earth plane. This is such a tender and sensitive subject, as the pain and grief that can be caused to loved ones left here on the earth plane following a suicide can be insurmountable at times.

When suicide spirits communicate with me, they do so with great difficulty. They may have difficulty communicating with a medium shortly after they have taken their own life. The grief cloud around them and their loved ones on the earth plane is enormous. They may go to a place in the spirit world that is especially designed for those who commit suicide; the soul cannot choose the realm where they seek to go. They will be taken to the realm that is most suitable for their needs at the time of their passing. Some say there are seven spiritual realms, and the fourth realm is the realm of peace and happiness. This appears to be the realm where a great number of people are directed when they pass over.

By committing suicide, the spirit has altered their own pathway of fate, and by doing so, they will have to return to the earth plane many times to work through their own karma. I do not believe that a person is meant to alter their own pathway of fate by taking their own life. Perhaps one exception to this rule is when a person is terminally ill and euthanasia has been granted.

After suicide, the soul finds that they still have extensive learning and great lessons to overcome. The spirit had felt that by committing suicide they would perhaps be released from the personal hell that they had experienced while trapped in the physical body. The spirit will still have many difficulties to overcome, and many of these difficulties have been created by the pain and anguish caused to their families.

They are often very regretful that they made the decision to take their lives. They may have committed the act and then decided that they wanted to change their minds shortly after the event, but sadly that was too late. They often hover above their bodies, trying to get back, but alas, the physical vehicle has died; the heart has stopped. They cannot connect back with their physical bodies—the silver cord has been severed. The silver cord is our spiritual cord, that which connects our soul to our physical body. Without our soul, our physical body is worthless. When our heart stops completely and our soul lifts out of our physical body, the silver cord, connecting us to the earth plane, is severed. Sadly, in many cases I link with spirit where there is regret following suicide.

In some instances, when a person has committed suicide, the family has commented to me after the tragedy that they felt it was an emotional release for all concerned. They are nearly always left with feelings of remorse, and always wish that their loved one could have been guided and directed to the help that might have saved them or guided them back to reality. The soul of the person contemplating suicide, however, is quite lost prior to the tragedy, and in considerable emotional pain.

When we lose such a loved one, we all tend to want to turn the clock back. When we have a strong love link, we have a hard time understanding *why* the suicide happened. Our healing process is so much more difficult and painful when we are left feeling that the tragedy could have been prevented, but wasn't.

However, God keeps us all in his light and can nurture any soul back to being able to receive spiritual love and joy. As family and friends gather together for the spirit's funeral service, they will be sending prayers and many messages of love that will help to bring healing to the spirit, who may still be feeling quite lost. These messages will reach the spirit almost instantly.

The love being received by the spirit helps to give them a stronger guiding light in finding their true self. I believe the power of love is the strongest form of healing and nurturing for those on the earth plane and those in the spirit world. Being able to receive this spiritual love brings balance and harmony back into each soul's life, and helps it find what it may have been seeking. Having made this decision to take their own life, the soul will come back to earth many times to work through the new karma it has created for itself.

Be reassured, however, that every soul finds love and peace in the spirit world. Family members can turn themselves inside out trying to help their loved one prior to committing suicide, but the answer is to hand the emotion over to God. When dealing with bereaved families of suicide cases, it seems a lot of these families often feel responsible for what has happened. The family member will ask, "Why didn't I listen to them more?" For one reason or another they were not able to prevent the suicide.

Often a person planning to commit suicide will contemplate the act many months in advance. It is important to remember, in any situation, we cannot live someone else's life for them. We can be loving and supportive, but we must allow that person the honor of shouldering their own burdens, for that is how they grow spiritually. The essence of it all is that we cannot live someone else's life for them. We must step back, otherwise we will fall down the well with them.

We tend to want to throw a lifeline out to someone close to us if they are in a deep well of emotional trauma, but often this results in their saying, "Throw me another rope, for this one is not long enough, or it is too wide, or it is the wrong color." The final request is, "Please step down into the well with me." When you have reached this point, then you know it is definitely time to step back. Just pray for their highest good to join them in their well, then hand it all over to God, and they will be helped more than you could ever imagine!

The feeling of guilt after a suicide may greatly affect the remaining family members. We must guard against taking on this guilt; we are not reborn to take on guilt for others. I am sure, in most cases, that we would not have been able to turn the clock back or prevent the outcome, regardless of the efforts we imagine we could have made, and this next story is a good example.

I remember reading for a lady several years ago who had left her husband and young daughters, to live with another man. All her family had disowned her for doing this. The man she had moved in with was her father's funeral director. Her father had recently passed, and she had been very close to him. The funeral director showed her deep compassion, and they struck up a relationship. She left two beautiful daughters, a loving husband who was to undergo heart surgery, and a beautiful home, and now she was ostracized by her family. Her children were crying out for her, so you can imagine how distressed she was when I saw her. She was in great emotional pain and turmoil, yet she could not leave her new man.

On one occasion, she telephoned me in an extremely emotional state, and I drove around to visit her. When I arrived at her rented home, there was very little furniture—just a bed, a small table, and two dining room chairs to sit on. She did not have a car and walked several miles to work each day. She worked in a job she hated. For the life of me, I thought to myself, why is this lady putting herself through all this pain and heartache, let alone everyone else around her? But she was adamant that she would stay put. Of course, we all have free will, but I truly wondered about her situation.

Then she asked me, "Jenny, do you think Jack is going to die?" My throat tightened as I looked at her. I felt, yes, the man she had left her family for was going to pass soon, but I would never in a million years have said so. I looked straight at her and said, "Oh, you mustn't think that way. It is in God's hands, my dear, how long any of us live in this life." Even so, I felt while talking to her that his time was nearing. I had a strong vision that he would be in a truck or a van when he passed over.

Three months later she phoned me in a very distressed state to say that Jack had committed suicide in his van. Before his passing, he had even become a Catholic just like her, and he wanted her father's name in his naming ceremony, even though he had never met him.

Here was a case where, no matter how hard she tried to make his life happy, even by giving up so much of her personal happiness, always assuring him that she wanted to spend the rest of her life with him, a woman was unable to change the table of events that were to occur.

When a loved one passes over to the spirit world, they are given a guiding light to help them reach the spirit world. This guiding light helps those who have committed suicide and other souls find their way to the spirit world. I liken this bright guiding light to that of an angelic light; it is a light that radiates and is given to a person as the transition is being made during the severing of their silver cord. This light helps to pull the spirit from their physical body. We talk about the God light or the Christ light; I believe this light has the same divinity.

Being able to say good-bye to a loved one also makes the transition easier and is a special gift. We truly are blessed and privileged if we are given this opportunity. So many do not have the privilege of saying good-bye. Of course, none of us are eager to let our loved ones leave; we usually want to stay together. However, if we are present at a loved one's passing, by holding their hand and passing on our love and peace to them, we help give them the necessary energy that they need to help them make the transition between this plane and the spirit world. When we can give this kind of assistance during such an emotional time, we are thanked by spirit.

Even though many of us may know we will meet our loved ones again in the spirit world, or be able to speak to them through a medium or have a conversation with them in the sleep state, the time of transition is still a most difficult and painful time. I remember saying good-bye to my father at least a dozen times. "Go to be with God," I would tell him, as he was so ill. He would say, "I do not have to go to God; he is right here with me now." How right he was. My father was not going to leave until he was absolutely ready. I am sure that the permission family members expressed to him, when he was so ill, to leave the earth plane, helped him with his transition to the spirit world.

Saying good-bye to your loved ones encourages them, as a gift of permission or freedom, to be released and to move on to a life that takes them to a higher dimension, one of love, peace, tranquility, and a higher learning.

After the soul makes its transition, it moves on to a spiritual plane or dimension. In fact, we all choose our spiritual plane.

The spiritual plane that we join after we leave the earth plane is determined by how our lives were conducted down here on the earth plane.

If we walk in the light while on earth, it will be much easier to reach a higher plane. If we focus on a pathway that is corrupt, then our plane in spirit will be cold and unpleasant. It all comes back to the saying, "What we reap, we sow." This applies not only in this lifetime, but in our life hereafter.

Our rewards come to us according to how we have lived our lives on earth. We create our own heaven and our own hell.

I liken the earth plane to being in the first grade; we come back to learn and to progress. The earth plane is our school of learning. It is my strong belief that the earth plane cannot be destroyed for a long time, if ever, as we need this plane to keep coming back to, so that our souls will continue to evolve.

CHAPTER SEVEN

A Helping Hand

I HAVE BEEN GIVEN PERMISSION by Debbie, who received this reading, to write about it. I saw Debbie in April 1993. She walked into my room, and I felt a grey cloud around her. However, as far as she was concerned, her life was going along just fine. She didn't have any real worries.

At the time of her reading, as far as she knew, all her family were all fit and well.

I asked her, "Do you have a brother in spirit?"

"I do not!" was the shocked and abrupt reply.

I gathered from the tone of the reply that I was very mistaken. I quickly continued on, always looking for the positive for her. We all have too much negative energy that enters our lives, and I believe a reading should always bring the client peace, joy, happiness, and tremendous upliftment, so that when they leave the reading, they feel as though they have been touched by spirit. Many people would not recognize this feeling per se, but they would certainly say that they feel different afterward. Many people gain tremendous healing from being in the company of a medium.

By now Debbie's dad was communicating with me and telling her not to worry about her brother Bill, that he was looking after him, and helping him, and that he was in good hands. She could not understand this message, and after the reading she went away feeling a bit bewildered by it all.

A few hours after she returned home, she received a phone call to say her brother was with a hunting party in the bush and that he had failed to meet up with the group and the helicopter that had dropped them into this remote part of the bush.

"He will be all right," she told her husband. "He is an experienced hunter and knows the terrain well."

She continued, "But something puzzles me about the reading I had with Jenny today. She said dad was looking after Bill and that he would be all right—and she asked me if I had a brother in spirit."

"Oh my God," her husband said. "Deb, do you know what this means? It means Bill is badly injured or has already gone." These words Debbie refused even to consider.

She felt in her heart that Bill would be all right. A large search was mounted, for several days. Many, many people searched for Bill and could not find him. Finally, a private search mounted by family members and Bill's friends found him. In fact, Debbie's husband Mike actually found Bill lying in a grassy area beside a stream. He had passed over several days prior and was in spirit at the time Debbie came for her reading. He was now safe and well on the other side. He was a strong person and had a very strong and loving bond with all his family, so it was a sad loss for them all.

When Debbie phoned me before they found Bill's body, I said to her, as I would say to anyone in this type of case, "Never give up hope." She needed to see her brother's body before she would actually believe he was gone.

I later received an exact record on tape, given to me by Debbie, of her reading, which she wished to share with many.

The following is a word-for-word account of Debbie's description of the sequence of events:

I'd been to see Jenny on a previous occasion, mainly out of curiosity and to see if she could contact my father, who had recently passed away. I had gotten so much out of the reading that I made another appointment ten months later. Settling myself into the armchair, it was only a matter of seconds before dad was in contact with Jenny, relaying messages. It came through very clearly that dad was getting quite agitated trying to get a message through to me that I just couldn't quite understand.

Later on listening to the tape in view of the events that were about to happen, it all became so clear.

Jenny said, "Your dad is giving someone who is very close to you a helping hand at the moment."

I couldn't think who it would be. She went on, "Have you a brother in the spirit world?"

I replied "No," but added that my father had a brother in the spirit world, Uncle John.

She asked, "Were you really close to him?"

I said, "No, not really." I wasn't much help, so we moved on to various other things.

Then Jenny came back with, "I can see someone. He's tall, has lots of messy hair, and is wearing a coat, something like a jacket, an oilskin jacket, and believe it or not, my dear, he's pulling out his pockets. To me he's saying, he's broke, he's broke, all the time."

I laughed and said, "Yes, I have a brother exactly like that."

Once again Jenny went on to other matters.

Ten minutes later she comes back again, "Oh, my dear, the person your dad is helping is so very, very close to you. I'm getting a name, oh dear, what is it? I'm getting William, christened William, but you call him, you call him Bill."

"Yes," I said, "I have a brother, and he is called Bill, and when dad was alive, he was always giving him a helping hand, or more like a helping handout. Dad's probably worried about who's helping him now." Anyway the reading ended with me coming away thinking, well, I didn't get much out of that one!

That evening, just after dinner, the phone rang, a phone call that was about to change my life. It was from the Gisborne police. Bill had been hunting in the Ruakumara Ranges for the last week, which we knew, with two other companions. The party had split up four days ago and were to rendezvous at Bill's base camp, at two o'clock today, to meet the helicopter to fly them out, but Bill did not turn up for that rendezvous. Grave concerns were held for his safety. Shocked and stunned, I relayed back to Mike, my husband, about the reading I had had with Jenny that day. I said I felt that Bill was lost, and dad was helping him to find his way out.

Mike listened to the tape and with great fear in his voice sat me down and explained, "Bill has hunted in the area for five years in a row. He knows the area like the back of his hand, and when you are in the middle of the bowels of the earth and you know the only way out is by chopper, you make sure you are there when it arrives. After listening to the tape, Deb, I feel Bill is either very badly injured or he's dead."

A team of fifty search-and-rescue workers were sent in the very next day. We travelled down the following day and were based at a sheep station called Marta at the foot of the Ruakumara Ranges. They called it Operation Marta. The next day, forty more search-and-rescue workers were called in, along with an army mobile kitchen to cater for the rescue team. Another day passed, and a team of specialized dog sniffers and their handlers came. Another day and a Television New Zealand camera crew flew in to follow the events. Another day and we were flown in on an Army helicopter to be shown the area and the conditions in which he was lost. Another day and another day, and still no sign. Finally, a decision had to be made. One more day, and the search would be called off.

That day came. We left before the field workers were called back in. An indescribable and unbelievable feeling sat in our hearts as we drove away with no Bill. After a day of being home and after missing a week's sleep, we gathered all the energy and resources we had to start our own private search. My family, my husband, his hunting companions, and thirteen good hunting friends of Bill's set off. They were flown back into Bill's base camp.

Mike and a helicopter pilot found Bill the very next day. He was lying down in a beautiful grassy area, next to a stream. He was wearing an oilskin jacket. The autopsy report read that the approximate time of death was between the first and fourth of April. He died of extreme hypothermia. Bill had passed over when I had my appointment with Jenny, and I do believe our father was giving him a helping hand.

A few months later, Debbie had a second reading with me, and her brother Bill did not waste any time in coming through and telling us about his passing. He related the fact that he had an illness at the time of his passing and had not been well for some time. This was suspected by Debbie.

He showed me his skin, and it seemed to be a darker color. It was very patchy looking. When Debbie saw Bill's body, due to the length of exposure, he appeared quite dark and his skin was patchy. He showed me his bare feet. They were all swollen, so he had no need for his boots, which, it turned out, the family had tried to squeeze his feet in to, but to no avail.

He gave Debbie other personal details that were important to the both of them. I believe he planned to be found by someone he was close to and loved, and that was Mike, Debbie's husband.

Debbie has no doubt in her mind that her brother Bill is happy in the spirit world and is fit and well. In fact, she talks to him a lot herself. She misses him terribly, as does the rest of her family, but she knows now that he is with their father in the spirit world and is very happy. It was his time, and he chose the place he loved the most, a Garden of Eden setting, in which to leave his body. They say no one is closer to God anywhere else in the world than in a garden.

I am ever so grateful that Debbie had the courage to come forward to record these events for me to share, as I believe this is a perfect example of proof of the life hereafter, and that when it is our time to pass over, someone from the spirit world will always take care of us and lend us a helping hand as we make our transition.

True, the family will go through their grieving process, for most people don't get over the loss of a loved one but simply learn to live with it. However, the more we can free someone and let them go to their progress in spirit, and the more contact they have with us to give us reassurance that they are indeed alive and fit and well in the spirit world, the more we can continue on freely with our lives here on the earth plane.

CHAPTER EIGHT

Sharing Past Experiences

DURING THE PAST FEW YEARS it seems that I have continued to meet an increasing number of people who are seeking to discover and connect with their spiritual pathway or increase their spiritual awareness by way of a private reading for the first time.

All of my private readings are provided in total confidence, with only a taped copy being retained by my client. However, I have been given permission to share the following past experiences with you, as a very brief sample of the beautiful experiences that I am privileged to share almost every day of my life.

The readings that follow have not been identified for their mystery or wonder, but rather to provide continued proof that messages received from spirit might be simple, but they are always messages of truth and love.

Son and Father Reunited

Margaret was an alternative healer and a very warm and gentle person. Her mum, Irene, was visiting from out of town, and Margaret suggested she come along for a reading. We had not met before. Most times I do not remember a reading, as I am just a channel working for spirit. But some readings where people come to link with loved ones who were tragically taken, or other sad cases, I do remember. This particular reading did not seem to be out of the ordinary to me at the time.

A few months later, I received a phone call from Irene asking me if I remembered her. Of course I did, and I also remembered some of the information that had been given to her in her reading. At that time she had shaken her head, and in a negative manner actually made me feel that the information being given to her was quite wrong.

During her reading, she was told about a man in his mid-forties, olive skin, brown eyes, and dark hair, who lived overseas and was connected to her husband, Harry.

"He is a very successful businessman," I said, "and you will get news of him this August and meet up with him in November. There is great joy ahead at this meeting."

She shook her head. "I can't think at the moment who this person could be, Jenny," she said. "We have a son and he lives in New Zealand. He has blond hair and blue eyes and does not fit this description."

Unbeknownst to Irene, her husband did have a son living overseas, from whom he had been parted for forty-five years. Later, when Irene phoned me and asked if I remembered her, I did, of course, due to her denial about this young man who kept cropping up in her reading.

As it turned out, her husband had been married very briefly to an Italian lady in the second World War. They had become separated during the war. The woman was pregnant and had a son. His name was Abbey, and it was Abbey's and Harry's greatest inner wish in life to find one another to link up.

At this time, Harry was not experiencing good health; he was getting older, and he prayed that he would one day meet his lost son and be reunited with him.

Unbeknownst to Irene, Harry had placed an advertisement in an Australian magazine sponsored by the Salvation Army that tries to locate missing people. It was through this advertisement that Abbey's aunty spotted the article and made contact with Harry in New Zealand. She had located Abbey in Italy but had arranged a surprise meeting in Australia.

Irene's phone call to me about the olive skinned, dark haired, brown eyed young man came in August. It was in November that the secret meeting was to take place.

Abbey was a successful businessman. All this information was given months in advance to Irene, and she was overwhelmed with it all. When Harry and Abbey met, they had an instant bond and told one another of their love for each other. Neither of the two men had ever given up hope of reconnecting. Abbey brought his family to New Zealand for a holiday, and everyone got on extremely well. After forty-five years, father and son were finally reunited.

I greatly appreciate Irene for sharing all this information and providing confirmation of how the spirit world gives out so much useful information to so many.

I say to those who question or mock this work that through readings, many people are given hope, strength, guidance, and faith to trust in themselves in a positive and loving manner, and the experience just enhances one's spiritual pathway via sharing the light and linking together.

When I hear such feedback, especially in special and loving instances of confirmation such as Abbey and Harry's, it leaves little doubt that there really is a life hereafter. I can only ponder the thought that if everyone were to report back to me the proofs and confirmations they have received as time passes after their readings, the evidence of the validity of the messages and of survival after "death" would be overwhelming. This, coupled with the fact that the information I am given from the spirit world is usually privileged information that I could never possibly know about or have been able to discover, is again living proof of the life hereafter.

Millie

I have been given permission to share this story, but I have not used original names, out of respect for the family connected to the incident.

A lady of about forty years of age, whom I shall call Anne, came to me for a reading. She was very tall and slim, with blonde hair and blue eyes. She had a calm about her and appeared very clearheaded. She certainly was very attractive, and she spoke with a very serene tone.

The reading commenced, and her life seemed in balance. Her father was in the spirit world, and when he made his presence felt to me, he began apologizing to his daughter Anne, who was seated before me. She showed no sign of emotion, however.

Anne's father was apologizing to her for what had happened. Something was wrong. I could feel it. He had passed in tragic circumstances, and I felt that his life had been taken. From experience I have learned to tread very carefully in situations like this. I must exercise the utmost degree of sensitivity in all matters connected to a loved one's passing.

Anne said, "Tell me how my dad really is."

"He is telling me that he is fine, my dear, but still has some sorting out to do."

He passed on some further information to her; then, out of the blue, Anne said, "Well, Jenny, can you tell me if Millie is with my father?"

This sent a cold shiver down my spine. "Oh no," I replied, "she is here, but she is not allowed in. The guides will not let her in to talk to me, and she is definitely not allowed near your father. Millie is standing behind a door. I can see her, but she is not allowed into the reading."

All felt cold and dark around Millie. This sent shivers down my spine. This had never happened to me before. Never had my spiritual guides refused to let someone into a reading.

As I looked at Anne, she sat calmly and looked me straight in the eye and said, "Good, Jenny. I'm pleased she is not with my father, because she shot and murdered my dad and then turned the gun on herself." Anne continued, "It has always bothered me that she may be with dad in spirit."

It would have been easy for me to tell Anne that Millie was well in spirit and with her father, but this would have been far from the truth, and I'm sure that this young lady would have doubted the authenticity of my clairvoyance if such a message had been given.

Proof could only be shown by relaying an accurate message.

A Trip to England —Betty

When I first read for Betty, I could see her husband in spirit, standing very close beside her. Betty was near retirement, and her husband, Harold, a tall handsome man, had suffered a heart attack while swimming and had drowned. This was some eighteen years prior.

Harold told me that he was determined to help Betty while he was in spirit, and he told me that Betty was going to sell the family home and move into a lovely home that she would like so much better. The new home would have smaller grounds and be more manageable.

Harold went on to say that the change of home would enable Betty to take a trip home to England to visit her mother and other members of her family, whom she had not seen for over twenty years.

Betty's reply to all of this was, "Not likely. I'm staying put. I love my home, and although I would dearly love to go home and visit my mum and family, I can't see how I could ever afford it."

When I saw Betty some eighteen months later, she told me that everything Harold had said, had happened. She had gone away for a few day's break not far from town, and when she came home, she had picked up a real estate paper, not really interested, but her attention was drawn to one house in particular.

She decided to inspect this property, loved it, put her house on the market, and sold it a week later. As she had some spare money from the sale, her son said to her, "Why don't you go home to England to see grandma and visit the family?"

This is exactly what she did.

It is always so good to hear from people who give me feedback and confirmation, especially those stories that have a great deal of joy and happiness attached to them. This is one of the biggest rewards I can receive from my work.

Betty was able to go home to England and visit her mum, after having been separated for twenty years. I am sure that her husband Harold, in the spirit world, played a big part in helping to arrange this sequence of events.

Jean's Son-in-Law

Jean, a psychic lady, sent her son-in-law, Kevin, along to me for a reading. Jean felt that because he was family and she was very close to him, it would be better for him to have a reading with someone he had not met before. I also feel more comfortable reading for people I have not met before and do not know any details about. This cushion of non-familiarity really brings home the accuracy of a medium's work and how well they are tuning into the other side.

After Kevin's reading had concluded, he remembered a very important message he had been given concerning money. He was told during his reading that in approximately two years' time he was going to be offered the opportunity of sharing in a syndicate that chose numbers for a weekly lotto draw. Kevin was also told that at the time he might not have enough money on him to participate in this syndicate, and that he would have to borrow twenty dollars from a work colleague. The advice given to him was: do not refuse this invitation to participate in this weekly syndicate, as you will win some money, and it will be at a time when the money is most needed.

Kevin was not in the habit of gambling, but when the offer came to join a syndicate some two years later, he thought it would cost him only two dollars, but realized that the draw covered a ten-week period, thus costing him twenty dollars.

Because he had little money on him, had a wife and family to support, and was finding his material pathway a little difficult at this time, he did not really want to gamble. However, something made him recall the message he had received two years prior. He decided to take a risk and borrow the twenty dollars from a work colleague.

It was with great joy and celebration that he was able to phone Jean and tell her that his syndicate had won first prize in the lotto draw. There were about fifty people in the syndicate, but he still ended up collecting about five thousand dollars. To someone who didn't have a lot of spare cash, that was a lot of money. He reported to Jean that since the family car had broken down, he was able to repair it, sell it, and buy a better family car.

I believe this message helped the family out in a time of need. From my many experiences, I have found that spirit generally only gives messages about money, or brings money matters up, when that person is in need, or genuinely needs guidance.

Tiria —Off to England

I was giving a reading for a lovely Maori lady whose name was Tiria. Tiria was a well-presented lady who had a warm, motherly presence to her. She was very soft-spoken and carried a warm smile. She had been a secondary school teacher for a number of years and was in-between jobs when I saw her.

Tiria had a great understanding of spiritual matters, and she spoke to the spirit world herself often, receiving her own messages of guidance.

On the occasion of Tiria's visit to me, she felt she could not get her own clear guidance through and wanted to hear what the spirit world had to say to her through a medium. Very quickly, her grandfather came in very close to her. When I am working with a very close love link, I will see an apparition of the spirit flash in front of me; usually the spirit is standing behind or close to my client when this occurs. Often I will see that the spirit and my client have a close family resemblance.

The spirit always gets my immediate attention when showing themselves to me this way, rather than clairvoyantly, where I see them in my mind's eye. Tiria was from a family that had a lot of *mana,* or power, around them, and her grandfather wasted no time in appearing before me as an apparition.

She told me, "I have so many questions to ask the spirit world."

Her grandfather did not waste any time in giving me a message that she would be travelling to England in three weeks' time. She laughed out of surprise and disbelief. Tiria did not believe a word of it.

She had very little money and thought this was a huge joke, although she said, "I would love to go."

I must admit I was rather surprised when spirit told me she was on her way to England in three weeks' time.

Again she laughed. "I'm flat broke," she said.

She left the reading very amused at this piece of information.

Two weeks later I received a phone call from a very excited Tiria. She was so excited that she could hardly speak.

"I'm off to England next week, love," she told me, "I cannot believe it. It is true; my grandfather wasn't having a joke with me."

Here was a lady who already had two sons in the spirit world, had helped so many people already along her pathway, and had now received a special phone call from England.

A few years ago, she had adopted a boy who was abandoned, a street kid, and she raised him for a number of years and cared for him. This boy had grown up and gone to live in England. He had trained to become a psychologist for six years and had married a lovely English girl who was a nurse. They phoned Tiria shortly after her reading.

The adopted son, who called her mum, said out of the blue, "Can you please come to England for six months and mind our five-month-old baby girl? We are both so busy and need some help at this time. We would love you to come and be with us. I've posted your ticket in the mail, and I hope you can come, mum."

Within three weeks, she was off. The other funny part of this story was that when she was told by spirit that she was going to England, she said, "I have no money."

I was given the reply from her grandfather "Don't worry about it, dear, it will all be taken care of."

And it was. This is a lesson that we should never doubt, particularly when it comes to having faith and trusting. Money is a circle. It comes in to us and goes out again. Everything is always taken care of for us by spirit in one way or another. The lesson so many of us have to learn is to have faith and trust in ourselves.

Healing —Raewyn

It was early one cold winter's morning that a young lady called Raewyn came to my door. Raewyn was an attractive young girl and about twenty four years of age. She carried very little weight and looked very pale and thin.

She did not have an appointment with me, and as I opened my front door and saw her standing out in the cold, trembling, she looked very distressed. She looked cold and tired. I was still in my dressing gown, but quickly gathered her inside and placed her beside a heater to warm her, while I went off to get dressed.

She asked me if I could give her a reading, but I felt she was far too distressed for a reading. I suggested that I offer her some healing, to which she agreed.

"We'll leave the reading for a few weeks, love," I said to her, giving her little snippets of reassurance as they popped into my head.

She had just broken up in a serious relationship with a man who had shared her life for quite some time; she was unable to deal with this separation and was extremely depressed.

I asked her if she would pray with me when I placed my hands on her shoulders to give her healing. She said as a child she was belted if she did not pray, and this had caused her to go in an opposite direction. She agreed to pray together, and as she was receiving her healing from the spirit world, it was as though her inner light was being turned on again. After our first healing session, I saw the color return to her cheeks. It was after our third meeting that I realized that spirit had managed to turn this wee girl's spiritual light on again and allow her the warmth and confidence to continue with her life.

I believe that when she prayed, she opened up her heart and soul to the power of prayer and linked into her inner faith. She was asking and seeking help so desperately, and, through her prayer, Raewyn received the healing she required.

I learned from this experience that if ever someone came to my door seeking my spiritual love, I would never turn them away.

Jacquie—Being Prepared for the Life Hereafter

I have very strong and vivid memories of one experience I had when I was about twenty-seven years of age. One particular office job I applied for in Rotorua led me to meet a very special person, a lovely girl called Jacquie. This led me to a very strong spiritual experience that has stayed with me for many years. I was to learn later that I was put in this job perhaps to prepare Jacquie for the life hereafter.

Jacquie was in her early twenties, a beautiful and wonderful girl. We worked well together and enjoyed each other's energy. Jacquie always saw the funny side of things, and she had a great sense of humor. I suggested we exercise and go swimming together at the local pool, which we did many times. Our jobs were very busy for both of us, and we were both under a lot of pressure at times. One day an idea just popped into my head, and I suggested to Jacquie that she job-share with her sister and spend time with her sister's two-year-old daughter, whom she loved. Jacquie was trying unsuccessfully to have a family of her own at that time, so she jumped at the chance to work a four-day week and spend time with her niece. They would play music and dance whenever they were alone together.

Something came over me, for after the suggestion was made I couldn't help thinking it would have been nice for me to job-share instead, but that idea soon drifted away from me.

Little did I know that Jacquie was only to be with us a short time longer. She showed such interest in all my reports of spiritual awareness, and after my group meeting every Monday night, she would always want to know any information that I could share with her, and of course, there was always plenty. She used to rub her hands together and say, "So what exciting things happened last night?" Her big blue eyes always widened as she asked the same question each Tuesday morning.

The week of work before her passing was unusual, to say the least. Two days before she passed, I walked past her early before work, as she was sitting in her car with her sister. I was going to rush up and say hello, but something stopped me, as I felt their time together was extremely precious. On Jacquie's "last day," she was saying her good-byes. She did not know this con-sciously, but subconsciously a great many people, before they pass, spend special time with their loved ones.

We were having a conversation in the office this day, a spiritual conversation led, as usual, by myself. As I turned to look at her, she appeared to me to be translucent, just like a black and white negative photograph. This distressed me at the time, and I didn't say anything, but this was the first time I had seen someone appear to me like this.

She had told me that because it was Easter and a long weekend, she and her husband had decided not to go away on the busy roads. She felt it was too dangerous. The day before her passing, I parked my car behind hers in the car park, and she had to ask me to move my car so she could leave. She said, "Good-bye, have a great weekend."

I said, "Good-bye, love," and my last words to her were, "I'm not going to let you go."

The next day, the date that coincided with my tenth wedding anniversary, Jacquie and her husband and a few friends had decided to camp on an island on Lake Rotoiti. During transportation of Jacquie and two others, the boat they were in capsized. She was not a strong swimmer; that is why she had tried to strengthen her swimming skills.

Her two companions swam to safety, leaving Jacquie in cold water by herself. To this day, her body has never been found.

I developed a closeness with Jacquie's mum and sisters, and they asked me to do the flowers for Jacquie's memorial service. I had dabbled a little with flowers, and my husband Rob's mum, being a florist, had passed on a few tips.

It was so important to get this large flower arrangement just perfect for Jacquie. "Just leave it to spirit," I said. It felt as though this large arrangement of flowers was symbolic of the love and sunshine that Jacquie wished to pass on to her family. As I discovered, when I saw the flowers up front in the chapel the next day, they were perfect. The florists from spirit had come in the night and put the finishing touches to this arrangement.

Ever since that time, Jacquie has visited me from the spirit world while I have been in the sleep state, and I know she is happy and fit and well. It makes me feel privileged to have known her and shared with her.

Jacquie tells me she is happy and is busy looking after the spirit children. The spirit children's ages can range from babies to young toddlers. Their wee souls are loved and nurtured by those who have been assigned as spirit mothers in the spirit world to care for and love these children. She has even appeared to me in a maternity dress, and I felt she was telling me that she does not have to worry about having children any more, for she is now a spiritual mother to all children. I saw her smiling and very happy.

In fact, I have often spoken to people from the spirit world while in the sleep state. They have not all been love links of mine, as is Jacquie; however, some have been friends of my family. Each time they come, they always have a warm and contented message to pass on. They always appear to be very happy, often giving thanks for the lovely service they received, or just giving thanks for the friendship and love they received from different people. There is usually always someone around me to whom I am meant to pass this message on, and I always feel privileged to do so.

A New Life for Mary

Often when I have met with someone whose circumstances are very sad, I have the wonderful opportunity to meet that person again, after six months or even a year, and find that they now have happiness in their lives.

One such case was a lady named Mary, who came to me in such a depressed state that she could not even hold up her head as she walked down my front path. She felt she had very little to live for.

As I commenced her reading, her husband came to me from spirit and started to make a wonderful communication. Then, to my surprise, a young lady stepped forward and told me that her name was Judy and that she was with her dad.

"We are both happy, mum," she said.

"That's my daughter, Judy," Mary cried.

Judy was excited to be in contact with her mum and continued to tell me about her son, Aaron, who was here on the earth plane.

As the reading progressed, I learned that Mary had lost her husband to cancer, and even though she herself was only in her early fifties, she was taking medication for a heart condition.

The death of Mary's husband had been a tragedy for the whole family, including her daughter, Judy, who was so distressed and depressed from her dad's passing that she had committed suicide by taking an overdose of her mother's heart pills.

As if this double passing wasn't enough, I found from the reading that Judy's young son, Aaron, who was two years old, was in the legal custody of Judy's brother, and he would not allow his mother, Mary, any time with her grandson. Mary had been very close to her grandson, and so this situation was extremely devastating for her.

Judy came in spirit to tell her mum that she was sorry, and that Mary was not to blame herself. Judy said she would like to have been able to turn the clock back, but she reassured her mum that she was at peace and that all would be resolved happily very soon.

Judy's message to her mum from the spirit world continued. Mary was told that she was going to meet another male companion, a thought that couldn't have been farther from Mary's mind, especially in her circumstances after the loss of her loved ones.

When I met Mary a year later, my Christmas gift to her was a reading. She was so much happier. Her life was starting to come together. Her son, who had custody of her grandson, was slowly dealing with his grief and letting go of his anger. The best news was that Mary had met a delightful gentleman. He was a motorbike enthusiast and had a motorbike with a sidecar.

Mary giggled and said to me, "Who would have ever believed that at my age I would be getting around in a motorbike sidecar? We laugh a lot, and I feel sixteen again."

She continued, "Jenny, following my first reading and my being able to communicate with my husband and daughter in the spirit world, I felt as though I could again hold my head up. I now look forward to living my life."

Bless her. I was so happy for her.

Andrew

I wish to share an incident that involved my old school friend and maid of honor, Andrea (we call her Andi), when she came to Tauranga with her family for a visit. I was out at the time she rang, and so she left a message on our answer machine. I hadn't heard from her for some time and was very excited to return her call at the hotel where she was staying.

When I dialed the number given, I asked to speak to Andi. The lady who answered the phone sounded stunned that I had asked for Andi, and she paused for a moment.

She then said to me, "I'm sorry, you must have dialed the wrong number. We had a son called Andrew, and we called him Andy, but he is no longer with us." She explained that their son had passed over some years ago.

This took me by surprise, and I apologized. For some reason, I told her that I was a clairvoyant, something that I do not normally do. In fact, I am not in a habit of shouting my profession from the roof tops, even though I have longed to do so on many an occasion.

As I later discovered, the phone number I had dialed and the number for my friend Andi were the same, except for the last digit. I thought about this telephone conversation for the next three weeks, keeping the number stored in my mind. I felt the need to phone her back, as I felt her son Andrew around me in spirit, trying to make contact with her, and I knew I was not going to be able to let go of this until I had made contact with his mother again.

My second phone call to Andrew's mum resulted in her wanting to make an appointment for a reading. This was her first opportunity to visit a medium, and I was happy to be able to link with her son for her. We had a lovely time. Andrew had passed over as a teenager, and I feel it was very important for this contact to take place.

Andrew's mother received a lot of emotional healing during the reading, which I believe she required.

It was rather beautiful how this was all planned by her son from the spirit world, and I am sure it was the start of much new awareness for her.

Craig

Early one morning as I lay in a deep sleep, I was awakened by a ringing sound in my ear. I tried to ignore the sound and make it go away, as I lay drifting in and out of the sleep state. "There it is again. I wish someone would turn that jolly bell off," I thought to myself. As I placed the pillow over my head, I soon realized it was the telephone ringing. "Who would ring so early in the morning? Well, they will have to wait."

My spirit guide Amos had different ideas. He whispered to me, "You had better get out of bed and answer this call; it is very important."

The voice on the other end of the telephone sounded very distressed. It was a lady whom I had met on several occasions when she attended some of my workshops. "Jenny," she said, "something terrible has happened. My ex-husband, Craig, has just lost his beautiful fiancee in a car accident. We all loved her. He is in such a bad way emotionally; can you please help him? He feels he wants to die also."

She went on to tell me that Craig's family was very concerned and worried about him. He was unable to eat or sleep. Craig had never had anything to do with the spirit world, and she did not know whether he believed in the life hereafter. I reassured her that people do not have to believe, but I felt it would be a good idea if she could bring him over for a chat. As we ended our phone call, she said she would try to bring him over soon.

I felt a chilling sensation all around me and knew that his fiancee in the spirit world would not have any trouble making a connection with Craig, as the love link felt so strong. As I slipped back into bed, I felt a strong sense that Craig's fiancee would direct him to see me very soon.

It took Craig a few days to gain the strength and courage to contact me for an appointment.

The time arrived, and I took him down to the special room that I use for readings. Craig was in his mid-thirties; he was tall and had very striking features. Craig's brown hair was cut short and was neatly swept off his face. His eyes were an overwhelming color of blue. He looked pale and thin, but I noticed that his face had a shiny and healthy glow to it.

I could tell he was not interested in eating and had lost his appetite completely. He was trying to present a brave face, but I knew he was just going through the day-to-day motions of life. I just wanted to gather this young man up from the low stance he was feeling and give him spiritual upliftment.

Craig cast his eyes around the walls in my reading room, looking at all my portraits from North America Indian life by

Edward S. Curtis. "Do you like Indians?" he asked me.

"Yes," I said, "I feel a strong spiritual connection with them and have felt this ever since I was a child." I went on to tell him that I used to dream a lot about the Native Americans as a child. We could have discussed the subject all day, I am sure, but it was time to get down to the real business of why he had come to see me. After all, Craig's visit to me was in the hope that we could shed some light on his situation, which seemed rather dim at the time.

I said to Craig, "Just sit back and relax. I do not have any guarantees about making contact with your fiancee, but we will try to do our very best for you, my dear." "We" meant me as a channel and my spirit guide helping me to make the connection. The grief cloud sitting above his head appeared to be falling very heavily upon his heart and shoulders.

"Give me a minute to tune in, please, Craig," I said, as I urged him once again to sit back and relax. I closed my eyes and said a deep prayer, and it was not very long before Craig's fiancee appeared to me. "Craig, I can see her. She is so beautiful, her dark, shiny hair at shoulder length. She is so petite; she looks like a dancer to me."

Craig replied, "Yes, that's my girl, all right."

"She is coming in closer and clearer, Craig, and wants you to know she has no marks on her body now."

The tears flowed and rolled down Craig's cheeks. His fiancee was so very sad for having left the earth plane and her beloved Craig, but I could also see that she was surrounded with peace and looked so angelic.

As we continued, a breakthrough came, as Craig's fiancee whispered her name to me. "My name is Linda," she told me, "and I was killed in a car accident on my way to work." I had already been told that she had been killed in a car accident, but it was good for Linda to be able to tell me her name and where the accident occurred.

Craig let out a deep sigh as the tears continued to flow. Craig acknowledged the information being given to him. He looked at me with his big, blue eyes, his voice quivering. "I always used to ask Linda why she was in such a hurry in life. I am so laid back," he told me, "but not my Linda. Always full of life and energy and on the go, she was always in a hurry. 'Slow down, Linda,' I used to say to her, and she would always give me the same reply: 'Well, you never know, Craig, I might get killed in a car accident on my way to work one day.' Sadly, she was so right; this is exactly what happened."

This was a perfect example of a soul having a deep-set awareness of their own passing, and Linda wanted to achieve as much as she possibly could while living on the earth plane.

This type of message always brings home to me the message that we should always treat people in our lives as precious gifts—treat them as though it is their last day with us on the earth plane, for we never know when our time clock will run out.

The whole experience of connecting with the spirit world was a new beginning for Craig's very own spiritual pathway. As he thanked me and got in his car to drive away, I could not help wondering how much impact the spirit world had made on him. He was so depressed and had been told by Linda that he must not think of joining her in the spirit world at this time. Thankfully, Craig had a son from his first marriage; this gave him a purpose to go on in life. Craig had a lot of happiness ahead of him. Linda told him that she wanted him to meet another lady and get married. She had whispered to me, "Craig will be very happy; he will marry again and have more children." However, the timing was not right to impress this message upon Craig.

I knew Linda had been a strong guidance to Craig on the earth plane, and I now felt that she would be an even stronger guidance to him in the spirit world. She would help him to find his new pathway in life.

Several months passed, and I received another call from Craig. He asked if he could come to see me again and talk to Linda. "Of course you can, Craig. It would be my pleasure to try to connect you once again."

Our next reading together was more relaxed, and we had a lovely session. Linda was able to communicate once again, and Craig seemed to gain more reassurance and be happier this time. He told me how he had played his first tape every night when he could not sleep. He went on to say, "I would just switch the tape on and drop off to sleep."

Hearing this made me feel very humble. I knew in my heart that Craig was connecting with a special voice vibration that had been passed through me as a channel and recorded on his tape. It would sound like my voice, but the spirit world had made a vibration that was soothing and calming to Craig's soul.

I invited Craig to sit in on my development group, which he has done from time to time. He first joined the group saying, "I don't know anything about this psychic stuff," and now he is the first person to give a correct message. I believe Craig will follow a very strong spiritual pathway, and I am pleased that his beloved Linda is able to help him from the spirit world to do this. I am sure she will also work from the spirit world to connect Craig with another lady for his future happiness.

Gwenda

It was a lovely, sunny morning, and I was enjoying the peace and tranquility of working in our garden. The sun was shining, and the birds were happily chirping in the nearby trees. I was in my usual gardening daydream state when I heard my guide Amos whisper to me, "Go and check your mail box. There is an interesting letter in it for you."

I continued working in the garden for a few moments, and then curiosity got the better of me. As I cleared out the mail box, I saw a letter postmarked from the South Island. I opened the letter, and it read something like this: "Dear Jenny, I don't really know where to begin, but because I live so far away from you, I was wondering if you could help me with some direction in my life. My name is Gwenda, and I am a widow. My husband passed away eleven years ago, when I was twenty-nine years of age, and I have raised our two sons on my own ever since. I really would like you to tune in for me and see if you can give me some guidance." The letter ended with: "I am scared; my wings are broken or maybe shrunk. I feel I need to move on in life and look forward to hearing from you."

As I read Gwenda's letter, I heard a voice whisper to me, "Hi, I'm not really dead; I am around my wife all the time, you know." This sent goose bumps down my spine. I felt this voice belonged to Gwenda's husband in the spirit world.

I sat down and stilled my mind, turned on the tape deck to do an absent reading, and it wasn't very long before her husband was with me again, giving me information to pass on to his wife and sons. "I really want to make contact with Gwenda," he told me as his voice faded away from me. The next morning I diligently posted Gwenda's tape to her as quickly as possible. Gwenda phoned a few days later. It was lovely to hear from her. She told me how thrilled she was with all the information given to her from the spirit world and especially from her husband.

"I am coming up your way in the next few months," she told me and asked if I could fit her in for a reading. Before I could answer, I heard her husband in spirit say, "Of course she can fit you in." I always chuckle to myself when I hear spirit answer on my behalf.

A few months passed and I had forgotten all about Gwenda, when I received a telephone call from her to say she was in our area. "Can you please see me, Jenny? I need some direction and really need to talk to my husband in spirit." I knew that it was important to see her, so we made a date in two days' time.

As I opened the door to Gwenda, I could see that she was still young, and had tragically lost her husband at an early age. "Come in, love," I said to her, "and take a seat." As she sat down, I saw a man sit beside her. His face was covered with ginger whiskers, his hair was brown, and he was of medium build, although I must admit he looked slightly on the chubby side to me. I passed this information on to Gwenda, and she seemed quite overwhelmed by it all. She acknowledged that the description of her husband was very accurate. Gwenda told me that she was very nervous. I reassured her that it was perfectly natural to be nervous and that she need not worry or be anxious; after all, it was her love links in the spirit world that I would be trying to connect with.

Gwenda asked if she could show me a photo of her husband. I felt that would be fine, as I had already given the description of him that I had seen. As I looked at the photograph, he looked quite different to me. "Gwenda," I said, "he is carrying much more weight now."

Oh, good," she replied, "just like he used to look before he had his cancer treatment. He was glad he did not have to shave during his treatment and grew the beard you saw. He was very proud of that."

One thing kept puzzling me, and I relayed this message to Gwenda, "Your husband says that the day this photo was taken was one of the worst days of his life."

Gwenda burst out laughing. "What a day!" she jested. "Because my husband was so ill and we knew he did not have long to live, we went back to England, where he was born, for a final visit. This photo was taken outside a castle, which took us all day to find. Chris was feeling tired, and when we found the castle, all Chris could say to me was, 'You brought me all this way to see this old pile of bricks!' We laughed about it for the rest of our vacation."

We chatted for a moment to relax her, and before I could even close my eyes to tune in, I heard a voice say, "Well, come on; I'm ready; we haven't got all day."

"All right, my dear," I said to the male voice, knowing that this voice definitely belonged to her husband.

I said to Gwenda, "You husband is a great communicator; he doesn't seem to have any trouble getting through. Your love link together is very strong." Gwenda told me that they had nine loving years together, irreplaceable and happy years, and she felt very blessed and thankful for this.

"Well, my dear," I added, "you are getting a big Catholic blessing coming to you from the spirit world." Gwenda smiled as she told me that she was raised in a Catholic family.

I spoke softly to her husband in my mind and asked him if he could give me as much proof and information as possible, so that his beloved wife would have no doubts whatsoever about our communication. "Well, first," he said to me, "my real name is Christopher John; people call me Chris for short. I passed over with a brain tumor."

I relayed this message to Gwenda and she nodded her head. "I think I am going to cry, Jenny," she said.

"That's all right, my dear; you are allowed to cry. Let the tears flow forth so they can fertilize the soil and allow the seeds to sprout for your new growth. Letting go and releasing is very healing to one's soul.

"Chris is also telling me that you have a dear friend called Rose and that he wished to give her a bunch of dahlias."

"Oh, my God, Jenny," Gwenda replied, "they are the only flowers I can grow in my garden."

"Well, he tells me he wants to give her the color pink, which is the color of love, for being so kind and helping you so much. He also tells me that you have a dear, black and white dog living with you, and the dog gives you great comfort."

Gwenda laughed as she told me that the dog slept on her bed every night. As the conversation began to change direction, Chris also told me to tell Gwenda that he had their golden retriever dog, Wag, with him in the spirit world. "Tell Gwenda I have Wag with me," he kept saying. Gwenda's eyes filled up once more as she acknowledged her husband.

"Please tell my wife that I am so happy now and that I really want her to get on with her life. She is not holding me back, but I want to see her make the necessary changes for her own spiritual growth." I could tell from the beginning that Chris was a very spiritual man and had a good understanding of spiritual matters.

He went on to say, "Get cracking, girl, and make your decisions about moving and bringing change into your life. Otherwise you will stop the clock forever and never make any progress in your life." I felt the information being relayed was very important.

Gwenda agreed that she badly needed to hear this message from Chris and admitted that she had been stuck in her life for the past eleven years. She knew it was time to move on but had been too afraid to move from her home. Chris butted in and said, "You mean move from your comfortable rut!"—a man who said exactly what was on his mind.

Gwenda and I had such a wonderful sharing time. I knew that Chris felt happy that he had guided his wife to a channel to make his communication and give her reassurance and direction so that she would make the necessary changes in her life to allow a new life to begin for her.

Our loved ones in the spirit world do not relax completely until they see our happiness on the earth plane. To me, Gwenda's experience seemed to be a perfect example of this.

"Before I leave," Chris said to me, "tell Gwenda I am giving her a large bunch of red roses, and to please celebrate our wedding anniversary coming up on the twentieth of November."

Gwenda smiled. "Chris always remembered exact dates of birthdays and anniversaries. He always used to remind me of special dates in the family." As Gwenda left our home, we hugged one another, and I felt I had made a new and special friend.

CHAPTER NINE

Trusting Yourself

OUR SPIRITUAL PROGRESS depends on trusting ourselves. How many of you have made an outright decision, perhaps an important decision, one which you have pondered carefully? You finally decide your next move in that regard, when suddenly you share your decision with your partner, friend, or family member, only to be told they do not agree with your decision, and hence you reconsider and change your mind. Alas, often the outcome will not be as good as if you had stuck to the decision of your choice, the one to which you were guided.

Decision-making can be tough at times, but always remember, when deciding, our first thought or impression of guidance is given to us from spirit. Our second thought or impression is our own imagination, which clouds our intuition, or guidance from spirit.

Often, when we do change our minds, we really do end up regretting not staying with our first impression of guidance. Trust in yourself, and always search for the pathway that will benefit not only you but all the others in your life. The right choices reach out and touch our loved ones, friends, and neighbors in a positive way. Through our actions we can touch humanity with our kindness. We can ask and pray each day to become a better person, to see the light. To become engulfed in the white light and be able to share it, wherever we go along our pathway—that is the goal.

We are and have been experiencing some very troubling and stressful times, with great tests of faith. The wonderful experiences of becoming a spiritually aware soul are limitless. Each and every one of us comes to our pathway of awareness in life by trusting in ourselves, in our own inner guidance.

To walk the spiritual pathway we must have faith. It was my own realization of faith that enabled me to commence my work as a medium for the spirit world. Faith is the key that opens new doors and links us strongly to our pathway of a new spiritual awareness. One of the lessons that we come back to the earth plane to learn is to have faith, an inner faith that will allow us to trust in ourselves, tune into our own inner guidance, and be guided by a higher power.

We often find that "we are where we choose to be" on our pathway. Faith gives us the courage to make necessary changes in our lives and allows us to walk along our pathway of life in a much clearer and more positive manner. Faith allows us to walk through new doors with confidence. Once we accept our own inner faith, we see our lives flow forth; changes automatically manifest within ourselves and in all other areas of our lives in positive, loving, and uplifting ways.

Always remember, you have spiritual people, or those in the spirit world, who are assigned to each and every one of you. As individuals we are guided along our pathways, not always the way we think they should go, but nevertheless we are guided, and thus we have the expression, "spiritual guides."

Your spiritual guides will not make any of your decisions for you. As previously mentioned, your first thought or impression is from spirit; this is a guided thought and is always given to you with your best interests at heart. However, we have free will to make our own decisions. The purpose, again, of your spiritual guides, is to do just that—guide you.

Spiritual guides are not interested in the trivia of life, but are assigned to help you along your true pathway. They come with you when you arrive on the earth plane and are often on hand in spirit to receive you upon your return home. Our spirit guides want to help us make the most of our lives on the earth plane, teaching us that our wealth in life is not material wealth, but our wisdom. We are born with nothing and leave the earth plane empty-handed. The riches we take with us are wisdom and knowledge—and our strength of character, that is, how loving, compassionate, forgiving, humble, helpful to others, sincere, peaceful, moral, selfless, and so on, that we have been able to become through our efforts, experiences, and choices while on earth. To learn this, we have had to return many, many times to the earth plane. When we return to the earth plane, our spiritual pathway needs reawakening. As we begin to progress in life and continue to discover personal growth, we begin to listen to our inner voice.

Spirit guides give you strength in times of need, shower you with love and comfort, and always send you healing when you most need it. We receive many gifts from the spirit world in many ways.

The wonderful gifts we have in this life are our families and friends. The relationships with those to whom we are closely connected are designed to help us reawaken our spiritual awareness.

Always nurture your friendships on the earth plane with respect, sensitivity, trust, and love, and you will never be alone. So many of us lack confidence and self-esteem within ourselves.

We tend to shut ourselves off from others, thinking that we have nothing to contribute, when in fact, others may feel comforted or even honored in our presence. Think about it. Say to yourself, "I know my pathway has been tough, but I'm sure someone else out there, someone I could meet, has had it tougher."

Many of you have had dealings with people who appear selfish. It is up to us to show these people that as we give and give, often unconditionally, the joy is in giving and not receiving. Unconditional love always overshadows selfishness.

It is true that we often give to another what we wish for ourselves. Our thoughts are like that, too. Say of another only what you would think of yourself. Like attracts like. Love attracts love.

Whether your gift to another is materially or emotionally supportive, you will be rewarded for the work you can do for another.

When we link with spirit, the experience should always fill us with love and joy. Remember, nothing is ever beyond our reach, if we pray and ask for our guidance.

Be guided along your spiritual pathway, and always trust yourself.

CHAPTER TEN

Your Conscious Choice

IF YOU MAKE the conscious choice of a commitment to develop a greater understanding of your spiritual growth, then I believe you will be given new directions that will help you to open many new doors, to a life of happiness and fulfillment.

In today's world, many people have become caught up in their material life, to a point where they have lost sight of reality and the real objectives of why they have come back to the earth plane. They have allowed their material life to take control, often shutting out the true joys of living. Learning to trust in ourselves and letting go of this material world can be very difficult. It is possible, however, to have a balance in our lives and still follow our spiritual pathway. If we can place less emphasis on the materialism that has become so powerful and controlling in our lives, and have a belief in ourselves and our inner personal strengths, then we will experience a new understanding of this reality.

When you make a personal commitment to seek your spiritual pathway, spirit will assist, by providing light and guidance. This spiritual light will shine on all those with whom you come into contact, and it will give you the inner strength to walk this pathway. You will feel fulfillment in yourself when you share this spiritual light with others. You will live your spiritual life in the belief that others may wish to choose to share the same with you. You will be ready to pass on a warm smile, a smile that has the same message in any language. You will be given encouragement and strength through times of trouble and distress. Your inner faith will help you to draw upon a courage to trust in yourself. You will replace your fear with faith and step forward in life with confidence and a higher self-esteem.

You will learn to become a more patient person and to be more tolerant of all those around you. You will learn to understand that your spiritual doors will open when the time is right for you, as everything we experience happens only when the timing is right. For many, the time is now right to reawaken their souls to their spiritual pathways.

Simplicity is the key to this acceptance of your spiritual pathway. You need only pray and ask to be directed and guided to the pathway of your new awakening. When the time is right for you, it will all be taken care of by the divine power. We are often guided to other souls on the earth plane who will help us reawaken our memories of an awareness we once possessed.

As you progress forward on your pathway, developing your spiritual awareness, you will be working for humanity, always sharing the light and linking with others. We must all try to spread the beacon of spiritual light, to bring more peace and harmony to our world. We can all benefit if we live a life of truth and develop our intuitive gifts to assist in spreading the light.

We are only human; no one is perfect, and all we can do in life is to try our very best. If all else fails, we must say confidently that we tried our best and then move on to our next project. Do not dwell on the past, but learn from those experiences and move forward on your spiritual pathway. You will have no need to look back, except to acknowledge the lessons you have learned, taking only the positive from these experiences to draw upon in the future.

Your new-found spiritual pathway will teach you never to be judgmental of others, and always to look for the beauty in every soul you meet. We can never tell at first glance how much pain and suffering a person may have endured throughout their lifetime, so be prepared to share your light in any circumstance. We must try to be compassionate and caring to all those we link with in life. By seeking your spiritual pathway, you will be replenished with soul food, and spirit will always be there with you.

Once you make a conscious choice to link with your spiritual pathway and tune in to your innermost feelings, you will experience an inner peace and happiness, and feel protected. Hand all your worries over to the divine power. Ask for guidance and seek spiritual light. Feel the light filling your whole being. Feel yourself smiling from within, and when these feelings engulf you, then you will truly know that you have begun your spiritual journey, a journey that will help you progress in this life—and a journey you will travel in a light that radiates through the eyes of spirit.

APPENDIX

Letters of Love

I AM PRIVILEGED to have received numerous letters from people that provide confirmation and thanks for their readings. The following are just two examples shared, and they are representative of understandings and emotions that are expressed by many after their contact with spirit.

Dear Jenny,

I feel I must write to thank you so much for helping me. When I came with friends, I didn't quite know what I expected. I just felt so desperately in need of assurance (I suppose you could call it that). My husband, who had passed away six months prior, was somehow still with me. If and when I ever thought about the day this might happen (as he was older than me), which wasn't often, I always felt I would be able to cope. When life is jogging along and you are happily and luckily in a lovely secure marriage, bringing up a family, you don't tend to think a lot about the subject.

Although not overly religious, for there were too many contradictions in the churches for me, I did know in my mind that this earthly existence couldn't be the "be all and end all," and that there must be some overall "Entity" (for want of another name) and that we move on to another place to learn more lessons. It was a subject that my husband and I never discussed, although he used to say, "When your number's up, your number's up," as you told me. He also vowed he would never leave me and would watch over me, but since his passing I couldn't feel him at all, and this was upsetting me.

I knew you were talking with him when you picked up his character so accurately, his sudden passing by heart attack, the other factors and medication involved (he had diabetes), our three lovely sons, my placing the house on the market, even his watch, which I had quite forgotten about, and so many other facts. You even mentioned his cooking. He was a chef in the Merchant Navy at one stage and did most of the cooking at home. (We compromised. I did the lawns, as I hated cooking.) You even took me to task about not eating properly. I am trying harder now, but I can tell you that learning to cook at fifty-one can be rather daunting, especially when I have to eat my own failures.

My husband used to tell everyone that I would boil an egg for twenty minutes to soften it. It was so good to know he is not suffering pain now, as he certainly had his fair share during our life together. Though I still miss him dreadfully, I've learned that grief is a very selfish thing. It's ourselves, the ones who are left behind, who we are sorry for. It is a very real, physical pain we suffer at not having our loved one around us, or at not being able to go into the next room and have a cuddle, as you so aptly put it.

I am very lucky, though. I have many friends of our boys, who treated our home as a base when they were all growing up. All still visit and help me, proving the old adage, "You reap what you sow." It makes one feel very humble.

I am writing this at three in the morning, one of the nights when my body clock isn't telling my mind it's sleep time, and as I reread, it appears too much "me and mine."

I don't mean it this way. I was rather trying to express just how much you helped. I can now laugh at some of my memories and realize how lucky I was to have had nearly twenty-nine years of happiness and fun with a husband who told me and showed me every day he loved me, even when we argued (as all couples do). He would say "You're a bitch, but I love you." As you picked up, he had a wonderful sense of humor, and there was certainly never a dull moment. Yes, I can even curse him for leaving me such a floundering mess. How could I have thought he would not be around watching my struggles, if only to get a good laugh?

So, Jenny, once again, thank you for all the comfort you gave. I do hope your vacation was all you wished, that you had a good rest, and were able to recharge your batteries. Your work must take a terrific toll on your energies. You have a very special gift and give so much of your own warmth and feeling to people. May you know great satisfaction on helping others like myself.

With Heartfelt Appreciation,
Ginge

Dear Jenny,

Thank you once again for a most enlightening reading, which you and I shared on 14th January. I'd like to come again later in the year. Please let me know if your phone number changes.

However, what I wanted to tell you was that you described and named my father, Alan, who died in 1939 when I was a teenager, but who remains close to me in memory.

An amazing occurrence took place this afternoon. Remembering that you had recommended I listen to music, I looked over my collection and selected a set of "150 Beautiful Melodies," which are fifty percent classical. Suddenly I remembered that my father was particularly fond of one classical tune—what was it? I looked through the list of composers and—yes—it was by Schumann and—yes—it was "Traumerei," which was on record four, side two. After all these years, I had remembered!

I put the disc on the turntable, noting that "Traumerei" was track six out of nine tracks. I lifted the arm, which immediately whisked out of my grasp and came down at the beginning of track six! This has never happened before—every record automatically starts at track one. You can imagine how I felt; it was uncanny, and shivers went through my whole body.

A similar thing happens with my husband's favorite song, "The Last Farewell," by Roger Whittaker. It always comes over the radio when I'm a bit down, such as on Christmas Day, 1981, just after he passed on. This song also contains the words, "I have no fear of death; it brings no sorrow," so that is comforting!

I've since remembered that "Anne" was my father's mother; I met her only when I was a baby.

Thank you again and bless you, Jenny.

Yours sincerely,
Shirley

A Rose seed will sprout into a beautiful
Flower. As our hands hold the flower it
Eventually dries up. If you crumble the
Dried rose into your hands and let the
Wind take it away, we can see that all the
Bits and pieces came from one flower.

If you took a white linen canvas and
Painted a white rose with soft hands
Holding it, all you would see is a hand
And roses at first glance, but it
Represents the spirit of God, the
Canvas they are printed on represents
Only one beam of light.

May the Christ-light that guides
Us all shine on your path and bring
You peace

Sue
1994

About the Author

For several years, Jenny Crawford has given personal readings in New Zealand, Australia, the U.S., and Hawaii, using her gifts as a clairvoyant, or medium.

Jenny first became aware of her spiritual gifts at an early age and joined a development circle at eighteen, at the invitation of Elma Farmer, well-known New Zealand and international medium, who now resides on the Gold Coast of Australia. Jenny further developed her gifts with Maureen Chapman, again, a well-known New Zealand and international medium.

As a medium, Jenny works to bring people proof of *life beyond death*. In her readings, she serves as the "middleman" between the spirit world and those still living on the earth plane. The spirits may provide valuable information to those who have requested a reading, or they may simply offer comfort to family and friends, offering positive and strong reassurance to help these people along their pathways.

Jenny likens her communication with the spirit world to listening to a voice on the telephone or hearing a radio broadcast. By clearing her mind, she receives messages from the spirit world in the form of strong thoughts and detailed images. A clairvoyant, she says, receives perceptions of spirit through the subconscious. She works both clairvoyantly and clairaudiently: clairvoyance gives the medium the ability to see spirit, and clairaudience enables a medium to hear spirit.

Clairvoyants are widely consulted, and spiritual societies are well-attended in the United Kingdom, Australia, and New Zealand.

In *Through the Eyes of Spirit,* Jenny explains that mediums communicate with the spirit world. For that reason, mediums often are able to provide some proof of the source of their information, such as detailed descriptions of a departed person's mannerisms, physical appearance, or a name.

Jenny's personal readings are hugely popular in Tauranga, the North Island city in New Zealand where she resides. She is generally booked six months in advance, and encourages her clients to have their readings tape-recorded to take away with them. Absent readings are also frequently given for people in New Zealand, as well as people from overseas countries, including Australia, Canada, England, the Isle of Man, and the United States of America.

Jenny has also been involved in a considerable amount of platform work, or working in front of large audiences, and she finds this very rewarding due to her ability to reach a large group with clairvoyant messages from the spirit world. In these situations, Jenny has the opportunity to provide proof of the life hereafter to many people at once.

Additionally, Jenny has organized seminars for the past few years for large groups, inviting guest speakers and covering all aspects of psychic and spiritual teachings, with an emphasis on simplicity. Seminar days always include clairvoyance by Jenny and are based on healing and on teaching people to raise their energy levels to "share the light and link together."

Jenny believes that all people have innate psychic powers, but most of us are simply too busy or distracted to develop our gifts. Through meditation and regular practice, people find that their intuitive, psychic, and clairvoyant abilities are strengthened. One goal of Jenny's workshops is to connect like-minded people, so they can form development circles that will give them the support and discipline needed to enhance their spirituality.